THE MESSIANIC TREES KIT ROBINSON

SELECTED 1976–2003 POEMS

ADVENTURES IN POETRY

Cover image by Hélio Oiticica from his *Metaesquemas* series
Gouache on cardboard, 540 x 660 mm, 1957
Courtesy of the Ricardo Rego Collection, Rio de Janeiro

Book design by *typeslowly*

Printed in Michigan by Cushing-Malloy, Inc.
on Glatfelter Natures Recycled paper

Parts of this book have appeared in some of the following publications.
Many thanks to the editors.

26, 6,500, A Hundred Posters, Abacus, Aerial, Aentonym, Anabasis, Avec, Big Sky, Combo, Disturbed Guillotine, Five Fingers Review, Gare du Nord, Gnome Baker, Hambone, Hills, hole, Jimmy and Lucy's House of "K," LetterBox, Long News: In the Short Century, lower limit speech, Lingo, Melodeon, Mike & Dale's Younger Poets, Mirage/Period(ical), New American Writing, 0/2 an anthology, o·blek, Occident, Poetics Journal, Prosodia, Roof, Sal Mimeo, Search For Tomorrow, SHINY, Sink, Skanky Possum, Strange Faeces, Terra, The Bay Guardian, The Los Angeles Review, The Provincetown Poets, The Silence, The World, This, Tramen, Verse, Writing, and ZYZZYVA.

The author would also like to thank the publishers of his books:

Barrett Watten (This Press), Geoff Young and Laura Chester (The Figures), Lyn Hejinian (Tuumba), Michael Waltuch (Whale Cloth), Steven Farmer (State One), James Sherry (Roof Books), Peter Ganick (Potes & Poets), Manuel Brito (Zasterle), Lyn Hejinian and Travis Ortiz (Atelos), and Simone Fattal (Post Apollo Press).

Thanks to Ahni Robinson for invaluable help in producing the manuscript.

Adventures in Poetry titles are distributed to the trade through Zephyr Press
by Consortium Book Sales and Distribution [www.cbsd.com]
& SPD [www.spdbooks.org]

ISBN 978-0-9761612-5-7

adventuresinpoetry.com

CONTENTS

To Ahni,
Pa' gozar

The Dolch Stanzas

I

he and his friends burned them
then they went home
and looked at it again

they walked about a day that night
black blankets on their backs
they walked full of good piss

for them to hunt it down
was far and away
a black look

can one jump
onto a track that way
four said they were into it

six said so too
by the way
their hoofs were charred

II

my little red one has not
time but for to eat
and play with me

today no sleep at all
alight with what to do
on yellow back wages

tough against tonic blue
so drum on by all means
music ages old and go

let down the spread to
warm the back
look

scan and run down
the one to ten
in him beside her

so they say
and run up to do it
for now

III

put it away
he gave it to him
she thought it over

they ended up at brown's
little was said of
each and every one

at six the sun jumps down
little by little
in its place

and you can see into
what's left
of what there is to do

IV
it can move fast
she is said to have
seen it go once

once and for all
by the white way
it left out

her one look
far away and
out of the blue

to get from it
to her and back
is said to look

as white
when it is late
and you can see

V

the old eye can read
anything at all with
one little old yellow look

VI

I would pull if I got right
but am stopped
by the funny take off

then cold sleep I take
and drink and ride fast
where I sit

pretty well over the edge
I think best
before it starts

to hurt and wash clean
draw grow pull and spar
I is no where

VII

together or on
right
what works there

tell us what
would carry the bundle
through those dark woods

important universal
always holds
bring some

we want to carry
enough to eat
out of our hands

VIII

they keep a pretty gum
between them
it sings down in this well

they put cheap pants on
and hold their fly open
to help the light

make three circles around this
in time to black and wash
hot bricks in the wall

the cut starts up
among them
a laugh

never sit on those
first long rounds
they cry

IX

or why think
ask
try out new hold

if they sleep
just as off
as always

put it to them
like this
say

here
this want
to be clean

open
not done
wants to know

X

if it's got ten hearts
it will almost take off
with blood

if afraid
there's another door
in the tower

then is always before
no longer
than it is round

this is ten
come to think of it
who ever did think

not one or two
but big red
the fly

XI
she said
that man went
where I was about to get

she said the bus
stops and lets
her little girl off

the sun is light
green with hot
work

we eat
a hot dog
and go back to work

XII

how did these
get here I wonder
what's small always does

now come away
said a piece of one
once to please

upon that best
and warm hold
I will become only

and not take of
what's given
together or not

but come back
said the one
take a look at these

XIII

you stop only
to go
hard

against black wood
pull it down
into the cold saw

and get that
going again
which is sharp

so to cut out
so much crap
that's put up with

make this out
as just like always
and you'll walk to help

XIV

everywhere
they went they
let off steam

they let off
blue and heat
they wanted to carry you

who were they
they didn't tell me
(full moon)

one of them had
wide teeth
when he stood up

to be about eight
days old with light
(full moon)

XV

you have to pay
your tax when you
are found dead

many wish
to eat much green
before they rot

I have been one
to always bank
off the rim

as I said before
you can tell where
the old play breaks

backs and must run
down to even see
where you are

you yourself
not what some person
says it is like

XVI

when I try
to take a step
my foot lands

beforehand
like the ground
is just there

it's funny
you find out
you knew all along

XVII

off the pig
that robs us
of what we say

to each other
that should be small
and live

not that big
laugh about how
to sit and wait

for some high answer
to put down
what's plain and wide

XVIII

he washes her back
clean
every which way

he gets big
to carry her
around and around

under what is
they cum
inside a wave

XIX

I do not like
the way that fly ran
under the chair

those bushes pushed
through that fence
are enough

now songs want
my head back
where I sat once

I got up
and drew
the plan

XX

I was just
thinking you should
do right

because that guy
in the yellow car
is a cop

XXI

something for everyone
there is something for everyone
at the beach

in uneven lines
white water and wind
blows hair in eyes

seven faces
in and out of line
got tans from the sun

it is fun
to see them play
just like some one

drew a line
they play with it
and the eyes have it

to look at again
as many times
as it takes to see

XXII

when you get to where
you can roll and
see out

a number of
numbers show forth
on a kind of

sun
it moves back of
grey sky

to make your way
in each place
more clear

seeing not
dim by dint of
what's not seen

Dream

X-rays of the skull
of H. Diane Ray
reveal 4 cracks or
fissures in that skull
resembling fjords
in the jaw and crown.
These correspond to,
and were apparently
produced by, the 4
theoretical
breakthroughs by which Ray
revolutionized
science. What we have here
is evidence burnt
in tissues of bone
of a tremendous
activity, a
life devoted to
and consumed by
research into the
unknown conditions
of that activity.
The x-rays are large,
sheer transparencies;
lit from behind they
look like silver maps.

Down to the Bone

After the flood
the early gentiles
rolled in the mud,
abandoned the families,
indiscriminately
chased after & fucked
the forest women,
who must have been wild
indocile and shy,
suckled their kids
then left them to wallow
in their own shit,
whose nitrous salts
fertilized the fields.
To penetrate the great
forest the children
had to flex and contract
their muscles and thus
absorb those nitrous salts
into their bodies
in greater abundance.
Unchilled or benumbed
by fear of gods, fathers
and teachers they grew
robust, vigorous, excessively
big in brawn and bone
to the point of becoming
giants. Great skulls
and bones are still
being found.

7 Days in Another Town

Mesopotamian wind
blows the same way twice.

"Forever"

Two bullet holes:
one in the window
one in the arm.

"Something isn't happening
or isn't going to . . ."

Then, sun,
The Wedge

San Francisco, 1974

Dear Carla & Benny—

I had a refreshing and wonderful time in LA. Thanks for taking care of
me so well.

Carla, I have not written more for your & Stephanie's mag so am
sending what I did jot there with this scholarly annotation which you may
print too if you want—

Mesopotamian for the UniRoyal plant with its incredible Sargon of
Akkhad design. Also for Griffith's depiction of Babylon in Intolerance &
the fact that LA, like that metropolitan area, was settled by nomads who
had to come across desert.

Wind for that gale that nearly blew us off our feet & made walking to the bank an adventure.

Blows the same way twice (in fact, "forever") in Topanga Canyon where we saw aisles of stone raked up the sides of hills by the air off eons & crouched in curved saucer-shaped caves carved out by same—twice in contrapunction to remark of Heraclitus about not being able to step in same river any more times than one, his point being a universal state of flux, whereas in LA forms tend toward a monolithic eternal Idea, like the movies, or Century City isn't about to budge. "Forever" is what Chris Burden wrote inside the shape traced around his body when he fell off the ladder he'd been sitting on X number of hours.

Like I said the bullet hole in the window was really made by a pebble Larry threw up there to engage the attention of Rene Ricard who was inside talking on the phone. The force of the wind drove it through. The one in the arm is from another of Burden's stunts.

"Something isn't happening—or isn't going to . . ." was said by Rene Ricard on same Topanga drive in reference to sight of a small crowd, several vehicles, unidentified equipment and police milling around on top a bluff. I still don't know what he meant, specifically, but as I'd mistakenly assumed we were witnessing aftermath of an accident, possibly fatal, I took it, morbidly I guess, as a comment on death.

Then, sun, which continues to appear, especially yesterday here, and The Wedge where the surfers go in Newport Beach. Vico claimed the wedge was primal creative form, representing ether, which carves all creation out of air—hence first Mesopotamian writing used cuneiform.

Love, Kit

Entropica

a suite for Eric Dolphy

Golden State

> *There are twelve guys in town*
> *who'll go all night in just their shorts.*
> *They're going to go 41 nights this year.*

This guy has nothing to say. We might as well admit that from the beginning.
Anyone looking for that crucial wedge of information might just as well . . .

Mint smoke flaw he mused as he walked the full length of the apartment. His
boots sounded on the wood floor. Rain dripped from his overcoat and hair
in the grey light. He noted no changes in the apartment. He did notice, from
the front window, tiles inlaid on the landing of the concrete steps bellow,
shapes of leaves, a dull red on white, he'd never seen before. He might just as
well have been expecting tanks.

The frog does no more than extract flour from a white patch between its
shoulders.

All nature becomes to this man a vast animated body capable of passion and
affection. Wind whistles & water tumbles thru the gorge. Meanwhile the
human mind "takes" forms of that nature. Climbing out on the branches for a
look see.

You neither vomit nor excrete fire, and do not perish on a funeral pyre but on a bed of flaming cotton.

He was pleased by the delicate contours and brilliant colors until they informed him that what he was looking at was not a fungus but a stomach wound which had become infected.

The next morning they went up into the sky where they became stars.

Golden Future

Dear Cha Cha World War,

Rain falls like silk down. Frank Nitty gets out of a black Ford. Jean Simmons' leg quivers a little. A man stretches out. He breathes. Smoke glides. Feathers. It has been cool all morning. The toilet leaks. They have planted a bomb in his chest. An old woman realigns the stack of newspapers. She is superbly dressed. The kids are playing in front. Noreen wishes to be called "Marie." The man pours a dark liquid into a bowl of milk. He is preparing a poison, to poison a collie. Sun beats on concrete. I am driving an axe into this dark liquid.

Like minded brothers and sisters get it together.

You feel music coming up your spine. Music in Java. Red on a yellow ground.

Helicopters land on gutted building tops. Blue daze at the horizon. Shark's tooth. A street swept with beams.

Everybody seems to be breaking up. Rog and Stella. Hinton and Betty. Vera and Mortimer. Varek and Cagliostro. Rachel Rhodes and Clarissa. The Charmer and the Faceless Thing. Mr and Mrs Frank Buck . . . It's "that" time.

X says Y has "splinters in his eyes." Ashley was on cloud nine. She was gone. Long and wandering over the fields.

Winter

I figured Tokyo. What is the northernmost city. You didn't answer, said something I didn't hear. I stood in the Arctic light.

Dimitri raised diamond-studded knuckles to his chin, the walls of the room dusted with a fine brown powder.

Owl palm blades bent stiff in the wind.

It is California, and this California detaches from other, from any imaginable Californias. Tail wind to tail wind breaking the pace. Some hunters throw up a lean-to. Soft light on faces and tricky meals.

He explained that he had been hibernating, a curious figure which reminded them of the French speaking Indians at Sheboygan.

Battery history.

Which end would you say is up. Copper or wool. Water or gas.

You get to peek at the inner reaches of my soul, he said, out of control. Get the picture. A drunken stunt. The body is a picture—up front. Past you I get to a white wall.

A soft breeze that I took into my lungs from the open window beside me. It sized up to be about a six month cycle. I glossed the combinations as they cut loose and reformed, end, beginning, middle. All of my friends were there.

Pontoon

They eat only metal oatmeal and go barefoot in the spring muds. Their women are tall and reluctant, fashioning trails thru the mountain growth surely, intelligently, bracelets of teeth hung tight, a cool wind ruffling the lower grasses. Their men survey the borders from towers rigged of spliced bamboo, swaying in the crow's nest, thirty or forty feet up. The day is spent weaving line.

Signals delight. Down from hills to beach and then the Ocean opens out, fields of the deep, silver exposure from behind sky, wrinkled with light thereby, and vast, naturally, mounting to disgust, all fluid—seminal—until static planks in the deck are etched.

Their children are called monsters in the literature. They are more terrible than sound, breathing tin Gilas into your room in sleep. Red meat on forks of lightning.

It kept raining and the house floated off with us in it. It was our first civilized pleasure.

More terrible than bees.

The search party came in in crackles. High and dry, we were frisked, in caves. Holding naught. Sparks in the dried air of a father's story. It was back to the trailer, to mix the signals back down.

They stand, chalk blue, in the dawn light, the charcoal light popping orange slivers of late evening's fires, and they dance. Smoke rising in sections, back to where we are living, to dance, Green Domino, in the plumes.

Paloma

On this side of the street: African nobles, a bearded man in silk robes of yellow, maroon and magenta, a fez with metal insignia, long moon and star earring and a carved ivory walking stick. His wife in charged blue. A kid delivers a message, black nods and smiles graciously, youth ducks back into doorway, lobby of the Cadillac Hotel.

On that side of the street the kid has to thread his way slalom-style thru a line of security guards spaced evenly thru the forest. Guards are former U.S. Marines in faded green fatigues, square jaws, pinpoints of their shocked eyes in irises of watery blue. They are strong, but unable to co-ordinate their movements properly due to a loss of dimension. Each confrontation is a weird dance in which the kid finally throws his opponent off balance. Then proceeds to the next.

Would Mr. Rosselli be inclined to help in a program for removing Mr. Castro from the scene?

Columns of green rows receding to horizon with 8 spaced elms. Leve de Wereld. An ad for space. In series. In Venice, July, August. Each moment inches over into plenty of big Pacific Ocean.

Files play on Caviar of black rotting pomegranate. Sun on the concrete walk. The head, fine, the stomach brapping. Back to shower, chess and a number, saber-tooth tiger grinning from the street out front the Moscow METPO. Quick talk from 2 women downstairs, sentinel clarity falling. Down on the job.

Should we park in this space? The space of a long minute. Flanked by ardorous activity and sensation. 'It's discrete.' Now move it over.

Faded buildings back the beach. Paint worn squares. Benches spaced along a concrete boardwalk. Polynesian guy zips past on skateboard. "How is it?" We say All Right. Tuum Est. It is you. Azz Izz.

Key signature. Two Moors dropped into the bar. Two were holding, one moved up a solid third. Placement of discs on a blue western seaboard. Sight line to story line, can you read me? Pick you up at 8:30, wash of road noise, aircraft, sprizzle.

Swedish Ivy. Slid out the back window as the car rounded a turn. It was fine.

Viola Bells

Battery lamb. Take care of yourself. Fleet Stable. Aim for your mark. 10 questions. Having a mind spaces us constellations. Blink. A hot day with you.

A sense of responsibility motivates her to constant chatting, as if unless she 'keeps it going' everyone will fall into some kind of abyss. Ahni is otherwise. "We'd have to have quiet hour."

It is forbidden to taste the blood. Waking, mouth dry, sheets twisted. 1:05 pm, 2000 feet above Chicago, turbulence, sky a mass of dark and rolling features. Bent by sparks at certain edges. Paris highrise futures. In a bar at 16th and Valencia buying the right kind of gum. Mid-afternoon, total darkness outside on the street, we can walk right thru these walls. Convertible ride. The Stinker pulls my plug, I throw up a defense, life of piddling ease, am I out of line? His pleasant friend who's always right says yes I am. I shut up it's 3:15 Hetty tells me. I didn't know, thought I just got up. Tears for poverty and loss. She don't want to play it back, do I think we could go to bed? Her body strong and fully rounded, her skin smooth.

"I'll try to be outrageous as best I can. Paint my face every day . . ."

An old woman dressed in deep colors, the skin of her face tan, etched and finely contoured, a mass of grey twisted above it. Going to the store.

"He's like an anaconda," she said.

Vocals, Asha Puthli.

Serene

Runners stationed at half-league intervals along the high road to Cuzco run messages in from a thousand miles off.

The lake people, moving back into the forest, knew one thing, back into the forest, beads glistening.

Swivel, buckle, there was no way into it, carry me back to Old Virginia. Fancy french tire. I was a little disappointed in the panorama the motel. You grab a phosphate? Numb pan.

While he was peeing, a great clap of thunder. The Inca himself, from great fright, lowered his head till his left ear touched ground, from which blood began to gush, and suddenly he heard a great rushing of water beneath that spot.

Then the military music pipes up from behind the garage. White anteaters brew coffee in tennis ball cans glazed black over sterno. Burnt holes in yr shirttails. Homage Gastronomique.

From eating fish to eating deer and soon there were families.

A pleat in her dark kilt, rise at the base of her back, prickly knee surfacing to March thaw over wool tight sock turned down at the top. She wants some configurations to bring back. Air stitching coastal range scrub, stars up and out, a hum in her head, " . . . Over the Sea to Skye." Bring it in. Bring it on home.

Hear the pipes? Away off and nearing, breathing and no longer climbing, excited, at this distance, eyes wide, approximately three feet, I and I, breathing and storing breath to play with the fingers.

Ancient Germans dwelling about the Arctic spoke of hearing the sun pass at night, west to east thru the sea.

'C' House

A hole in the concrete wall was big enough, the sheriff said, to permit two adults to walk through it side by side.

Hot detail worked loose from nauseating blur.

Above him hung a circular balcony. Its base made of flat aluminum panels, a small high-intensity beam of light originating from every third panel. Above the base a simple railing of steel and wood and a narrow catwalk commanding a view of the bank floor from all sides.

A heavy sofa was knocked halfway across a large room, crashing into a table. Statues, lanterns, vases and lamps were toppled.

Standing in St. Louis.

There was nothing to do but wait on line. Customers will please wait as light flattens aspect. Great stainless steel safe.

14th & Broadway Oakland streetlight magnifying off glass bank towers to mark old municipal sundial at v.

Heavy damage was done to a large fireplace across the room, and an ornate Spanish gothic ceiling was shattered.

Dizziness, vague implausibility of random chatter, people tired, smoke, barely moving. Money. Ear and tactile sense of body as occupied space, the bull ring, rush of volume, sway, he falls down.

Every window was broken. Two doors on opposite sides of the building were knocked off their hinges.

Camera Obscura

w/ Ahni Barker

The cave people
come out of the cave
with their cameras

In the American Tree

A bitter wind taxes the will
causing dry syllables
to rise from the throat.

Flipping out wd be one alternative
simply rip the cards to pieces
amid a dense growth of raised eyebrows.

But such tempest (storm) doors
once opened, resistance fades away
and having fired all the guns you find you are left
      with a ton of butter,

Which, if it isn't eaten by some lurking rat
hiding out under the gate, may well be picked
up by the wind and spread all over

The face you're by now too chicken to admit is yours.
Wheat grows between bare toes
of a cripple barely able to hold his or her breath

And at the crack of dawn
we howl for more
beer. One of us produces

A penny from his pocket
and flips it at the startled thief
who has been spying on her from behind the flames

That crackle up from the wreck.
The freeway is empty now, moonlight
reflecting brightly off the belly of a blimp,

And as you wipe the red from your eyes
and suck on the lemon someone has given you,
you notice a curious warp in the sequence

Of events suggesting a time loop
in which bitter details repeat
themselves like the hands of a clock

Repeat their circular travels in a dreamlike
medium you find impossible to pierce:
it simply spreads out before you, a field.

Now you are able to see a face
in the slope of a hill,
tall green trees

Are its hard features,
a feather floats down
not quite within grasp

And it is Spring.
The goddess herself is really

Feeling great.
Space assumes the form of a bubble
whose limits are entirely plastic.

The Separateness of the Fingers in Trance

O how righteous, X, are all your days!
Earth blue jag scrapes heaping love glove,
Harsh descent drubbing puffball in
Wind blowing a scrap of paper against hot green.
The subject, meanwhile, of some interest at eye level

Vibration's masses door away, trembling
Thick with garbage and the dust of stars.
Flag steady. Heart of the minute.
O it is an interesting afternoon
Amid general hubbub ("Mambo!") touch of cold gringo scrotum

Like a truck through tiny lapses.
I am remote. Sky been to dusk aflutter. I drank.
Consolidate the Harvest of Exact Calculations!
With nothing to do for three months
Loudspeaker jabber over white-clad Louie Louie

Smooth morning troops hasten vertical.
We asleep. Jesus up. Sky the stuff open safely.
Stand back five paces and blow white side wall,
As light flickers from a point with abandoned machinery.
("I want to talk to you about that second Louie . . .")

She makes my heart work. Silence.
Dazzling puffs in station undertone,
Black rubber riddled & strewn. Sun. Drink.
The powers of speech are returning the ticket.
Since when? "Since right now.") is walking in.

Word thought all words white: back here and back back in.
And across the border, through the bad areas of the city
Sexual Copper. "Get off of my property."
Finance, strict back fast. My skin is dark
At a moment's ungainly notice. Sprinkled with water.

Back eye gets game born. Noodle grove at 28 km.
And you do not like this very much. So Far. The car
There's water on the parade grounds.
My head large and my clothes are nowhere.
Here is my corpse and there sits my patient mastiff,

The road itself looks like something that could talk
Stops at a house. Car bird finish is hand.
I, though out played daily, by stars simply outrun alone,
I'm pre-habit. My nails are plectra
Andante. Loathsome magma of my pre

And tell you which way to go, through green fields
Empty, it still carries the message. How many
Have learned at states' noise to field our machine head.
Along flightless birds of rain and moan habitude
Supposed and double sanctum stands to reason a day.

And trees, like a stray dog, to the canyon floor
Times have you heard an officer question a dog?
I prime freely what today consigned is here accorded surface,
Scuttled in favor of pinions surmounting eyesight
One and the same day in many places at the same time

And still not separate from itself, sky the limit.
Hang then above house tops. Place then lacks up.

As some drift off when lights are low mine does
You might as well spread a sail over a number of people.
I see what's that you say, recall in cold up tops,

Still emit faint glow over glass near empty and head
Enter above on pressure, place one foot up.
Have long heart, bald air, the sky has a tree in it.
Golden apples of our summer's work fumbling in the backseat
The green canoe-like beef tasted salty for days after.

Strong hat waves, waves motorcycles have anti-ravaged,
The western basins of the great continental chain.
"Into pitch darkness the stairs twisted and . . ."
Top back all 100 lights, red filters,
Bobbing high above what I suppose (light fog) to be

Tribute to Nervous

bottle-neck

oh I'd

humor my

behemoth!

tales

take

powder

pills

set sea

ordinarily

arbitrary

time of arrival

estimated as

The Channel

"The World's Greatest Assortment!"

ORANGE RICE

ATLANTIC OCEAN

The Novel

part of a trilogy

after an episode

based on fact

of Dante's Inferno

in London

in 1920

& so

snow falls

deep snow

further off

the train passes

behind a red temple

in the interval

is a correspondence

like across an arc

triumphant tranquil

mechanical take

all round

on the roofs

Turned Up

reasonably

opens window

cop car

closes, passes

well-to-do

nowhere to

be (STATUES) seen

green slopes up

to passing cloud:

"Let's get together and . . ."

flame (NOMAD) door

comes off

to take the bite off

ALL KINDS OF

angles

make a world you

"find"

it is located in

blue areas

about X% of the time

and to even have

a continent first

one came to have

a look

then put

OFFICE

FOR RENT

up over head

when phone rings

and they've got work for you

Not About

not to bitch or gripe a bit
you sentimental slob
look at iron
it is bad
to weep and moan
if you can't live
insert your head in
a metal drill press
so it cuts off
your head
That's right!
say you love
you let the cat out
the play begins
the play pursues itself
at the end of a hundred
and fifty pages
I'll be beat
the debut
has already been played
no one can change
the result

while waiting

I talk to myself

about the environment

in which the action takes place

it is difficult to describe

a red hat

I pass on by

four walls

you stretch them

I see in practical relief

heat stroke on far wall

vertical figure w/ diagonal top

and ghost image to left

grace catholic retinal red

to habit squeeze oriental water

in a glass of water

dominate but squeeze but simply

the side of the glass

morning after morning without one

knot in your head

I no longer know

where I am

at the same time

I write

I'm working on a book

locks open like a curtain

theatrical effect

an immense field of water

floating elevators

lift 500 tons

grain a day

days are dense

while I sit materially

where I sit

on account signed

by blank its blank

smokestack

Hole in the Don't

wonder what'll happen

one grey a m

jet noise filter's an

end to nervous systematic tune

coffee water then

coffee's in

order one

going on

upside down in

an apartment known

only as other than

light rain

about to begin

On the Corner

I want things.
You hear birds.
The heat is on.
Someone driving.

They have theories
to place facts
in an order.
They prove useful.

You all come back now.
He is the third person
to come in here
to answer the question.

Or she is
wary of his
possessive assertion
of theoretical fact.

Pages turn.
Why does the sound of them
credit such attention.
What listens to one is.

Steps on the floor.
He is absorbed in
his activity, apparently
typing something.

Imagine traveling
to different parts
of the world.
Jumps off boat.

Light blue map water.
Would money be available
on trees. Imagine work
or criminal exploit.

The prison house
of Latin. Pig latin
's granma. Hear tap
water drawn upstairs.

Present technology
porcelain punctuation
associative principle
pinholes via Joe Spence . . .

Writing writes itself.
I am not an animal.
I remember movies.
This is not an example.

Who needs obscure poetry.
What is the price
of cola product.
Why is reading such.

Now can anyone tell me
what question
I am asking you
said the teacher.

The sun goes down
into the town's
back pocket
like a figure of speech.

She calls her mother.
The other draws signs
at a table.
These persons are rhymable.

I is the other.
Having said that
is an ancient construction.
He split.

We live in a house.
I live in a room.
You stepped out of a dream.
You could have fooled me.

They made all kinds of money.
The long green. Great!
if you are reading this
in an airport.

Reader, writer, how
does the poem go.
Inner ear and eye
take a vacation.

I want to work.
He plays out the line.
You've seen this before.
So we meet again.

Riddle Road

Bright window shapes
the wall. Wet
leaves trace tree.
Broken walk. Book
or tree. On
the wall. Period
pieces together parts.
Traces halt error
dead in a
track. Window shapes
shadow a life.
Light wet leaves
turn night to
bright day. Grammar
moving has all
it takes and
gives up the
most. You can't
get out of
times had or
back back in.
True sounds sing
in standard English.

A feeling accompanies
equation. It lasts
while certain. An
action boxes fan
dates. Mechanical relations
obtain. Stop the
run off. Back
up. Where on
one roll may
perforations show up
I ask you.
Here and there
satisfactions rumple
the ground. Work metaphysics
into a small
craft warning and
form an address.
Colloquial suitcase second.
Two floor bed.
Two dozen jigger-capped
pints in walk-in
& red room.
The next word is
one over. Water
comes from space

to take air
apart. Moves take
time to come
and shape ahead.
Flat white wall.
Wet road sound.

A Sentimental Journey

White sheet moves on the line. Walkers, these are the songs, the senses, sentences.

Open the gate. Close up. Pickup truck drives by, aluminum rack in the back. Motor cycle starts.

Feet in the street. Shoes, newspaper, hands, the wind. Trees stock still. Sky with clock-shaped clouds. A pie in the eye slices the daylights on a weekly basis. Steam-proof headgear hyphenates the tongue. My father took me for a boy in a dream. I met a girl. The cars, the paint jobs, flowers.

The cult of intelligence. In an ordinary news story the frame doesn't have a leg to stand on.

Concentrate on what developing?

That everything is all right (not) is my dream concern. Agreement of merger, workers shred bosses. That a light goes on, my waking state.

| 22230 | 3.8 | $5 |
| 22277 | 3.8 | $5 |

Neptune's bridges' narrative pages. Selby: the diminishing room.

Met on the stairs and wondering (what to say) what to say.

Oh shit it's the idiot. Over there. I'll sit here like this. Just look at the sky. Selby's twentieth century, don't explain, places bets (words) here and here and here. A psychologist of the 50s. Despair, killing fucking time. Stop the clock. & Other Diversions. As staccato claxon sounds from Mission Street this moment your reporter and a tip and thanx to the hat in hand line of word, the line, playing out a hand. Time goes both ways, hands you a line. "Where I just came from . . . the fifties." Memory. Oh I'd. So Selby. Simple. Struck dumb by all those periods. He don't stop for nothin.

I want to rip history to shreds.

Think of a boot. Does it fit?

Thickness. I'll sit down.

To this: kids and dogs and a woman leaning in different windows. It's natural here. Humanly possible. Girls and boy are dressed (black and blue and tan and magenta) and turning, over the shoulder, to check each other out.

Guys shake (three positions) and concern themselves with cars. Guy goes up stairs carrying big L-shaped piece of plywood. Four cars are double-parked in a row. All actually en route & now slowly passing the first, a gold Cadillac circa 1960 w/ sharp fins, stopping to talk to the boy in the black windbreaker. Young white professional woman with leather briefcase and bag walks by. Guys fan out, girls crossing the street. Beep. Skinny ex-hippie couple nearly staggers along. Umbrellas in evidence, sky grey, but air dry. I'm cheerful, willing to entertain. There's the buzzer.

Flexible to a fault. Inconsistency kills self-justificatory disappointment in apologetic defense of optimism, nastily pointed.

Objectless abject.

Rode high for a week and on the seventh day I crashed.

Some of the more repulsive developments in avant-garde music are waiting for you in bed. Women check a form of address leering from a window.

The ice hung in sheets on the glass. The light came through it dimly, if at all. A slight breeze kicked over a hill of beans. Her hand moved lazily over the child, sleeping, the music of the spheres played as if from a punched roll scored by the pinholes stars made in the dark canvas bag of a sky, where the two of them lay in waiting, screening out random impressions in favor of intricate prints on silks and cotton cloth recently received from the orient. A bag of groceries floated up to the landing. There was coffee. The earth underfoot was solid, oozing with frozen fluids. He mentioned the air further south, how it felt walking along by the retaining wall, what birds there were there, and how he had set up some of the animals.

Eros pinned to the page. How impulse to write aligns with those to be alone, smoke, be stoned. Recall tree-climb as early instantaneous response of childhood thought to human event. From this perspective yellow flowers trumpet up into the air. Jet noise, red blank, bugs. Heat on the back, spigot. Here again a memory's a made trace. Making it over, pleasure to make over what's made. What world? The ant approaches the bowling ball. Jet noise echoes thought I saw a butterfly. In the corner of my eye, the sun. Our heat art in Oakland.

As much as I'm not able to control city spins against.

Peter butter and bacon.

The ability to operate machines is a pleasure. Still life. If I'm driving I know I am.

Mind moves in like a drunk.

Left right appears at sleight-of-hand wrong move, pitched forward in a seat.

Nomenclature hammers provided. Technicians wing X.

Often into clouds I look up from. Must be something you spoke. Not counting backwards. Club soda on table top. World. Fizz. Air in our era.

It's four and the morning. These stands for just what we see. The boats at anchor rock. Moon man picks up rock.

A transom has to open.

Green blades shadow the pages. Ink right across a line. Apply pressure to point. A little bit at a time.

Sun comes by the numbers. Body heats up by porcelain dump. Birds sing. Sage weathers fast break.

A leading tower of question.

Their attempts were always analytick: they broke every image into fragments. . . .

Club soda on sofa. Man stands boats into clouds. Simple git, ain't he? Tree-climb is a little early.

Rode high for a week to talk to the boy in the window. Retaining wall didn't get that. If I'm driving stock still I stop for nothing.

This ink makes the pages curl. According to the rules, accordions measure a pair of hands. At this depth, reader, the windows open. All whole air provided here.

Hear four cars double-parked in an ordinary L-shaped piece of news. The first, a bed, the second, a shoe, the third, memory. Paint jobs of intricate prints froze on the stairs. Guys shake (three positions) each other out.

Swallow a tin can? Could be a dream. Know how to whistle put two and two together.

Light tongues a flat white surface. Canny counter, your days are numbered. My hands are warm, my art larcenous. Days in the prow, skies go blue and white grey greens, leaves, shade the apartment. Hearty walkers, hello. Signs and waves.

He got out of his head (house) and hammered on the (?) roof. The car would be in fourth gear for most of the drive. Life in these United States wasn't what it once was (would be). Then they would get out of the car and walk a little.

Car talk, bar talk. Who gives good phone. Slice of rut. Tarzan's nuts.

Hear that motorcycle flak going away. Know a rap when you hear one. I back off of hype to hear the heater. A body away, talking to her mother. Most of the time there's traffic somewhere. Nearly any.

About face.

Leaves fall, revolution in the air. That saying makes it. So I go on down the street to Portugal.

Grass blows back on the median. 14 miles to pea soup.

Fatigue rocks the cavern of a word. We drive on up past State Beach. Trestle bridge. Flat Pacific blue beyond the tracks. White floats nearby and oil rig way out. Gaps in the trees give, light goes on, continuous drive states pass through nary a mumble. Cows by silent way, narrow bridge above floating birds.

I write. The draft was in my soup. Sometimes I want to split to where the pea meets the sky.

That's salt water alright. I've got a control with the other nostril.

A trivial death in the haunted house. Saunter over for another frozen banana. Old love boat is piracy, desire as skeleton mounted on heap of gold, orange light on paper (flames). A trumpet hangs in the air. Long trains of persons issue into the boats, others getting out, now dead? Lines line up to make false choice. Insipid, pleasant, and very clean. I like sitting on a bench, looking at people. The widest, mostly empty parking lot.

Emily Dickinson's C's.

Aviation and auto sound grind the day smooth. Day's greens spring between Santa Monica houses. O Delmer's Precision Brakes!

The brown hound is back.

Everything that happens can make a record be changing.

What you see is not the key it's what you say. Turn it over.

Walk. Heart.

GROW SOME BRAINS

An account of mind butting up against what's available. People know more than they let on.

Up in the mountains for a while.

Throw water at the sun.

CAR MORT

A shadow, a human form moves behind a window. Hands twisting something. Orange cloth spread with blue trim. Making the bed. Light bulb.

PARK

Park foot

Kids crouch, lean, drink, smoke. Guy rubs elbow. Sky. Vapor trail. This ink is thick. Bicyclist removes gloves. Keys hang from his belt. Friends hang on corner, sit on bench, wall above. One w/ T-shirt hung from back pocket, cap on head, gets on bike & tools around. They pass him a joint. Guys getting high, old guys walk by. Words to the girls crossing the street. Hands curl, come here, but they won't. Beard offers cigarette, hat has his own. Smoke. Three-wheeler motor cop. Bare-chested longhair in blue jean bells also has a can in a bag.

DELTA LINES

camera strap

Guy does pull-ups from branch of tree. Guy leans on parking meter. Other guy climbs tree & straddles limb. Hangs by one hand, drops to sidewalk. Knocks street sign pole w/ half-full beer bottle. Gets in car w/ buddy, drives off. Guys split, bicyclist splits.

An old woman approaches, walking w/ cane, in pale green overcoat & thin silk scarf, holding in the other hand the handle of a brown cloth bag and an orange flower. She lays it down on the step she's selected to sit on & reads a newspaper, the bargains section, leaning one hand on the wall of the doorway, edge of painted cement & metal gate. She pats her grey hair back from her face & rubs her nose. She is wearing black shoes and grey stockings. The bag handle hangs over her wrist, the cane handle likewise. Young blonde woman in orange dress slit at the knee, light green socks, glasses, passes & crosses the street at the corner, old woman watches her pass. One foot out of shoe now and resting. On top of it. Dog checks it all out from window.

In Oakland guys w/ white T-shirts and afros under hat & cap pour gas from giant can into back of silver Caddy, bring jumper cables out & attach to pickup engine. Slam down both hoods, touch brim, get in & go.

Asiatic bean pie. Hairnet. Thong. Sweat on the blocks. Bodies. Bandana over the eyes.

The nerves sit ceremonious who'll say I'm not. The happy genius of my household comes.

I'd leave music on but not the ball game. Sleeping Beauty meets Snow White. It is my habit. Numbers lead aisles down all the time.

I hung one brick. The rain came down. Not to speak was my sentence. The market for making every word count was a buyer's. Boy girls in black w/ hair dyed black & blonde. A shirt w/ parrots. The woman in line w/ the orthodontist. Correlations made the days sway. I spring 10,000 miles on the cloud trapeze. Back to where I can't say. Not knowing what market it addressed, the students made no sense of the writing. Walk into a room and start telling. Walk into a room of moors. Start yelling. For I walk along every day and it's not a job. I'm paying attention to a building shuddering in the wind. Wet glass ruffles, the leaves print. You don't know until you see it. Written down is placed, outside. The room where talk takes place is memory, just this side of the period. You can think this however. You want to stretch across the immediate space between daylight and waking. Space provides light with its one big opportunity. A bird on a wire's a high note. High-tops swing round in the intense inane: Gone with what wind?

He picked up the notebook to see what was happening. Time sheets spread-eagle.

Damned if it hadn't happened again and, this time, to him.

My eyes are the color of a mountain in Chinese.

He flips the sun visor up. She smiles and pulls away from the curb.

One cigarette for the past. A room in the wind. Private dancers take down a phone number. Aviation and autos sound out the window.

Mounted police straddles limb. Mother tongue is coated. Clouds cross the street. Random impressions hang from human event.

Real irritation is caused by broken lights. All broken, rugged and abrupt surfaces have the same effect on sight as touch.

The world exertion effort has reached a new high. Between walls, leaning back on a mattress, not seduced by the colors in California, they reach for a drink, magazine, embrace and roll against the open window. Downstairs a car speeds across the lot. Her arm, wrist braceleted. His hand toys with the loop of shade. Funny horn sounds in the street.

Old pink wall and smoke sun. A day's a place holder. I can no more explain than disappear. What all voices say I hear.

Wind that blows curtains and leaves is what clears the air. TV screen on at the back of a darkened room. Building nuzzling white sky. Dozens of images fly apart fast.

With this I'd put a hole in time. Heart face square. In the Columbus empire journal. Disarrangements of space, traffic squawks back, bright distance, clouds rush back of the action. This is a screen against which we moved. Movement from bush to bush, seething with fucking experience.

Do that over again.

How many times was the hand at the head, smoothing out the part. The head in hand part came in between. Part time work was out of the question, and to have time on the hands was not always a smooth thing.

An extra building darkened the white sky. An ordinary building darkened the white sky.

The police have blocked off the intersection as I write this with car and flares.

Mr. Secretary, will you read the minutes.

Work long hours to get a decent blur. Red and white lights at night. Round, in series, sound. Rhyming radios crash from the street below.

Street signs cross like Joan at the stake, lit up from beneath, orange, by the flares, pink, and flickering with the revolving cherry.

The blues is a grid. Random street noise, a shout or honk, lays in to 12 bars as voiced. Song is circular, frames history as variation.

Familial quintet in fetal hunker.

A headline is all we have time for.

The dance program I already threw away. Words in a sentence occur in some order. The next day I attended a meeting, and on the following day we took a party of girls to an island.

In a "Festival of Life" swarms of small creatures raised a terrible din, inciting and abusing one another, sometimes with a hint of some higher significance.

Variation comes into the sentence as thought displaces writing.

History comes into song, form turning on its round.

History leaps and bounds.

Days and the sun are round. Sound is the third term, makes a border. There is no identity in a sound world. The counter can come back to one any time and start over.

Cakes, bacon & up. On the counter. A bug is crawling across the calendar.

The creature has a purpose and his eyes are bright with it.

The earnest professionalism of German thought.

And tell me also when you will help me waste a sullen day.

By fever of reason stymied. An automatic voice produced these sounds. Thinking entered in on the last word. A scanning operation is successful when it locates an effective block.

Man fears desires to see, hear. Dogma produces edible shoe. Feet rhyme with street.

A game called stadium. Blue & yellow concentric plastic rings, descending to four holes in the center, each notched to contain marbles at regular intervals such that when a marble-bearing notch is moved even with a notch in the lower ring (or rings), the marble will roll down toward the center.

I live in the eye, and my imagination, suppressed, is at rest.

The very future is looking over a shoulder.

As if a very heart would break.

I have had great confidence in your being well able to support the fatigue of your journey since I have felt how much new Objects contribute to keep off a sense of Ennui and fatigue. . . .

JOE

We had a tolerable journey to Liverpool.

ALL FOURS

SONG

A SENTIMENTAL JOURNEY

Shade on leaves or grillwork on Division St. under the freeway. Pins on the line. I can only answer for sound, writing to you.

ALL FOURS

Two cheese rinds, a nail, a matchbook, THE BUILD-UP. Two Xmas balls in grass grown out around a spigot. One canoe, two paddles, one wading pool, overturned. Pool and canoe are blue.

Regulation sneakers have it. Causal tap remains entire. Guards named in affidavit. Ruins arrive by force of habit.

Non-reproduceable blue crossed out by "Big-Dipper." Bonded, birds can fly. Sing, wind, in sunny trees, a melody, for Mr. J.R. Moon.

The overplus. Human energy is great. I am waiting, as ever, for and with you.

A gigantic strawberry dwarfs our town. Bullet holes frame car length. The attendants go into the baths. All of Australia is watching.

Simpler butter rice needs but only sees. I'm touched by a wide assortment of types. Stations where shoes stand in array, diversion for the loitering uncle. The wind drove me across.

Desire drives the mesh. Age mates across the hall. Sleepers take it in, the smelt, the perch, the need to flounder aimlessly. Happily the sun, presently situated elsewhere, can be counted on to return the fingers to our hands, one by one.

Under the world lies a light blue cloud. Clouds are not real. Nothing is so sweet. Mind is a blanket. Dreams is a cup of coffee in the morning.

She washes mahogany leaves with mineral spirits. The trash has been burning for a while. You will understand, the wind is all about the house. It's a good feeling.

The surge: a stack of troughs.

Memories are made of baseball. Trip hammers correspond to striped bass. Association will take you to the ferry, fair weather or foul. Schools swim in circles, deep under presence of mind.

Baseball strike is off. Neptune's tomb is sealed with chains and padlocks. Sound of glass breaking, sirens, we see the Hulk, a combination of Steve Martin and Pete Rose.

While I arrange the alphabet elsewise.

Smoke and work. Out here in the field. Radio touch toes to childhood dreams. Kitty cat stirs price. Action unaffected by cord.

Two grown men searching, scrounging, shamelessly, for their medicine.

Vegetable letters.

When I wrote Dolch I was listening to Monk. The association of ideas is an old one. My desire in writing was to push logic out of shape. I still am.

Subjects swap objects. Playtime in California. A bird in the hand rolls snake eyes. Promiscuity states a case: private v. public. States on fire. Unemployed subjects seize high-priced appliances.

When I was a boy MADE IN JAPAN was a kind of joke meaning cheap merchandise. Mostly dime store stuff I remember. Now we don't hear that, as Japan produces most efficient automotive & sound equipment everybody wants.

Mind a wall of torn posters. How each new work modifies all that came before. That song again, after all this time (stuffing sleeping bag into stuff bag) marks that time, changed now.

It's what you want, thinking.

Stack the pace.

Sun on a rock, it eats your heart out.

Dream skin in a car.

Water, all the way around.

Head lights up. I sat down in my house and ate a carrot.

Songs are sentimental.

Oil menu. Roadside block. Cemetery arms. Hose games. Hand down the driveway. Light again. Home box. Watch tin face. Cereal up ahead. Darkness under the table. Cinder diner.

A leak in the sun is flooding any patterns. I've prepared a sketch. White out all dark areas. .

And there I'd sit and read all day like the picture of somebody reading.

The air has two different temperatures. Heard in the head, written in a car.

You have to allow for interruption. Jobs are continuous from birth. A boy crosses downtown streets to large apartments.

Temperatures are continuous from birth.

You have to allow for somebody reading. Jobs are boring, I won't read it. First pencil writing all day like the picture of a sketch based on a misunderstanding. Salt and pepper registered to vote in my place.

I hear a tune a guy's whistling outside. Words arrive in order, the writer is stationed, listening, the reader speaking silently.

Wind in the trees, I'll never get it all down. I remember coffee, sun on the leaves.

These tremors are useless.

The pain ball scudded across the day.

At night I don't want to give it up. The end of psychologism is jism.

The automobile drove to the photograph.

I've gone off on a tangent, but everything that organizes an individual is external to him. He's only the point where lines of force intersect.

Personal poetry has had its day of relative jugglery and contingent contortions. Let us take up once again the indestructible thread of impersonal poetry. . . .

Birds shadow a wall.

Grass pulls at the sun.

Sound folds support the wall. The air gives way.

A man or a stone or a tree will begin the last song.

Women stand out against an air.

I believe in breathing when a potato is being paid for.

Verdigris

The sign is a raw shape. People river. Space lights up the porch. Dust clouds the window. Ashes break down into sky. A bird flies parallel to slope of roof. Wires hang at a like angle. Comings and goings are frozen in the new room. Wind rooms in the street. Business gets complete thoughts down on tape.

Writing breaks off at mid-letter. Sound resumes. Shirttail. Waves heap themselves at your stone feet. The life of facts is undone in a day. That it organizes itself to work will identify the formality of the office. Three girls unite against a midsection. Paste-on stars glow in the dark. Bare legs, asleep on the floor.

Whatever became of thinking in a downpour meant a light on the stairs. Alternation. Big pattern. A shot full of holes. See-thru. Broken, weak, servile, sentimental, clawing at air. I'm seeing to you. Saying the number two to make it round. Grey white dock. Electron city.

The art of falling. There's more of a line there than you could let out. Trading fours. Candlestick and empty frame in the mirror Jack jumped. Squeeze yr knees into these. She listened for the sun to wake the birds. Things came to her indirectly by way of an echo from a canyon wall or the side of a ship. The telephone woke her through the wall. Political characters are held up by signs. Exposure is an enclosure.

Journalism is the tip. An iceberg depicted on postage stamps is set adrift. Edges, x's, zig-zag lightning, rips, wakes, cracks, canyons open on fact plains. Cool damp day fills in between Oakland and a chest of drawers, so I'm left to my own photos for a series of correspondences, cooking and picking out curtains. Clean lines. My vision is ok. Sound affects thinking.

One story leads directly to next. The deluded Don is a perfect cipher. Any reeds I office they start with greater care. The machine missed a stitch on this page. Corn dogs of ancient Britain. Lonesome whisper blow. Still laughs from a wake across the street. Sentences break. Down to material.

Plane noise more than it lets on. "Then how about our position?" Changes are infinitesimal or imagine a bird. Around the point rocks back growing light. The news's continuous, broken to bits. Keep active mind on long trips. The slogan is a model for how to write. You are engaged in the half of it.

A chill came over the freight. A brick wall registers to race. Spokes twirl in foreground. Angles are cut in the sky when I live and work. What music shows through double numbers. Wheels make showers that draw nowhere. Player piano roll scored by flight, birds above a west end theater.

Downstairs for a move. Animal spaces when staring into light we think. Complications are swept away by the foreground police. I reached for another, thinner slice of pie. Knit sweat.

Belly over arse sideways. Time between bubbles. The fourth makes these lines in a song. Noon habits clay bank hours in a collection. Red leaves made this table. Square holes form its surface. Wood laughs at facts because it's grooving. The light! end of side.

Clam falling, punk falling. Flame blackens brick. Ash breaks down into sky. It's wet out. Corrugated cardboard baffles. He pulled himself up by word of hand. Going through the door he found himself in another room, itself with a door in the far wall. Don't listen to this music the music seemed to be telling him. The world is made. It's a made thing.

Elements of style show through successive layers. Memory conditions rhyme. Interrogation aces line the precinct with scripts. If I were an oval no noise would come from the other side of the yard. A light bulb screws in slowly, lights up all at once. General electric patterns in a landscape. Stave the remaining heat off forks of lightning while I'm out. Range sequins. I inaugurate sleep.

Diagonal cross-hatch yields a diamond field. Numbers identify which parachute is falling from which balloon. Our first snow had to push wet light across the page. Cobalt to magenta, pea green to pink against space. Spear Street Towers. Be collected. To work push all this out of the way.

If you can describe it why do it. Cross-bred strains dot the map with an I. If these lines were longer I'd write them. What reason could I give to you. Singing: I've been far away. Pine cuts sky in three. Diagonal.

Of x of. Shoelaces, table, wood, the metaphors are all mixed up. Walnuts, paper, leather, talks sound back of a wall. The phenomenal field is history. A gear box is to shift speeds. I ran upstairs to write this then back down to pour coffee. Dreams perforate a waking state. People grow larger, take on more dimension.

Home from the war, the war at home. Revolving door gives onto electric eye, stableboy statuette. Way back in a cave shadows move on a wall. Shoulders take shape with greater care. Let's talk about Silver. I dig the trio sides. Gold light from bulbs rounds the corner. Ink blurts out well. These pages aren't stitched in. The subject is liable to fly apart. Striking parallels broadside.

Up to move. A car. The height subtracted space from a can. On all sides there were waste spaces with only stoves and chimney stacks still standing and here and there the blackened walls of some brick houses. A soldier on leave, a shirt outside pants. Barn doors open here on air.

Times square, space circles round. Past the boundary of self. A colored rectangle, longer in its vertical dimension, its surface void of detail, hangs suspended. Its edges, as if slightly raised, can't be seen past, form the periphery of the visual field. Motion a point near the telephone. Wall or side in a sea. Letters fell from tablets translated by tan. Words in the sky in the middle of the month. Diagonal slashes.

Pencil the attic. Bells chime in with the scissors. Light glances off chrome-plated cutlery from joy in Germany. Thus, an essay, trace, tale, nexus, gossip, plan. Any thing might do to flesh out space. Every metaphor is a fable in brief. Stripping foam off tops, blue pieces stuck to the wood. Put a bunch of names in front of them and they were. Air was invented somewhere above the street.

Walking between these sleeping people. An aroma, a texture, a tonality, a rap on the screen door. Stop something, it repeats. Lyrics. Spontaneous pile of rags. Screen door. Pierre stepped over the broken ground to the right, far away over the fields on which these men were floundering about, and there stopped, stood, sat, or lay.

Aerial wages piece about the sky. Over in a dream. Awake, a walk with the stars. Out, up, there, in, the sky. Rain on green slate and baby fir makes lines above the house. They brought play daily into the rope. There is strength in the overlap of many fibers. Letters fell from the word envelope. He took her legs on his back. She put his arms on his shoulders. The sun obscured them.

Trial de Novo

The writer is a mirror, the writing is a crack. Copy shop. Air surrounds the armed forces. Birds pierce the stillness. Notes scale down into rhyme. A song goes straight to the heart. Words said do later too. Off and on a feeling is stopped by a new tune. Words tone down the street. History repeats itself onto a master.

Change now tomorrow is another different day. Senses assume. Supports. Rave reviews crash against the steps. Lifted from water the infant knows less than it did. Workers organize the workplace by and for themselves. Jars light up from bugs on a state map. The light from the stars is a mine. Cloth flat on a shoulder.

People don't know what they're thinking about for half a minute. Polarity. Grillwork. A blue flame. Audible. Quick, thin, digital, hot, seizing right to acute. I'll be expecting you. Repeating the tune to a song on the window. Red drayage. Levee town park.

The bird impressionist. There's more to that line than meets the ear. Rhyming notes. Empty earth and full sky in the water follies proscenium. Accommodate yourself to this slum. She pays attention to the motors. What arrives comes little by little or all at once. A hole in the room holds the room in place. There may not be a car, but the mediator is laid bare. Place rhyme here.

Relief is supple. Politics is business in a taxi. The analyst is a fellow traveler. Cues, carpets, horns, hides, sounds at the bottom of the basement stairs. Holding my breath I air out the curtains which separate me from my neighborhood counting the current. Deal the climbs. When I see the glory. Sounds of a dime are hits.

One gunshot leads immediately to two or three or four. The casual bystander is a shoe-in for a witness. A book of photographs called evidence from different files. Agreement as to number can be problems. La Moore says Johnny Alexander popped her in the snoot. Heart in sweet surrender. Slipped the gun into a briefcase and walked back into the Tishman Building. A well-dressed woman. Up to no good.

Will will out another day being equal. Say something's made in Japan. Runover. I can only be responsive up to a point. A man becomes an infant again. Language organizes the world by and for itself. Alcohol consumes the space between California and Florida. In the light of my stars the stars. Pullover on soft shoulder.

A fever melts the tracks. A wing stays on air as a retainer. Gears mesh in background. Often I wake at peace with the earth in my gloves. That fingers push keys is a must. Darts tumble to moving target. Pictorials displace time and a half, go unnoticed until after an audience.

Up in back. Great to be borne on lives vicariously hospitable. Simplicity can hardly wait to take the floor. I checked the agenda for crabs. Eyes ring.

Pants zip up from ankle. Train time to stand stationary. The third is urge. Day parts stack up in an adverb. Warm bodies built this bed. Wide wheels roll it down the hill. Sound backs up light up to a point. The end of the line side.

Oyster rising, flaneur rising. Water lights wood. Patch a story together. Air is a different color. Science and memory in a box. She wrote every note of it. She opened the door to the office, went in, and chapter eight tells the rest. Light coming from behind the venetian blinds made them impossible to see. "Thing" is a fine thing. The world that was already is not.

Water rushes downhill to tell a story. Memory conditions fact. Police expert says damage is consistent with case in point. Maybe the anonymous caller was himself the hit-and-run driver. Information arrives in bits, gels in an instant. Particles collect on a file. Unhand the steps. I'd be delighted in sequence. I boy calms.

History states that politics rewrites space. Names combine in a series of red trees. The rain is fine, air all wet. Pounds to guilders, guilders to Belgian francs. Terminous. Tell us how it is you make of yourself a wall against the sun. Clear the decks.

What's needed's present definition. I had a sense of how to be in those towns. The last of the second, am I a moment ago? Fast actions are my greatest month of the year. Sizing: in bricks you hear. Language is a sand bar. Not music.

Make copy. Repeat, vary, derive, strike down, do what you canonical well please. The birth of capital, the rise of Venus, the heart of the artichoke, sounds back up over a yard. You're asking me some hard ones. To downshift, double-clutch. I wrote this in the mint. Metaphors are a dime a dozen. In the future we will not be around to discuss it.

Words in sleep made better sense. Bright day gives onto no such number, memory mere as a trace. Where these materials come from is immaterial. Reeds form the middle ground. Elvin cardboard sky. I love the wheel. Legs are modes, parting the reeds of form. Bells could eat a click. This page is taking days to write. The form of the instrument makes the song madrone, stronger than oak. Suffering suffix dash.

Up to heat up. A model. A revolving midsection glows in the dark office. No night of terror is as dark as this durable lacquer night. I saw a box with a picture of a seated woman selling cigarettes. What time tomorrow.

Voices print, emotional registers vote. Self is tacit. The prisoners, supplied
with rifles, pace about the yard, one crouching to fire into rock so the bullet
ricochets back killing him instantly. Another shoots his adversary, using the
other man's weapon, and prying open a basement window makes good his
escape. The subject a point on a screen, alive. Not waiting to move hand and
eye. Government lies, covers the globe with a false map. Words in the head
betray the active willing subject. Sun script.

Everything staccato of optimism. When workers seize the means of
production. Men and women rugged not seduced. New revolutionary
perspectives dismantle the machinery of oppression. Workers see these
words. Eyes open the world. My word—ground in a box! The wages of
death is work. I demolished 530 Bush.

Working amid these talking people. An angle, an edge, a chill, a flame in a
dark street. Start something, it repeats. Laws. Specific pile of tires. Dark
street. Now you have to see the enemy and draw a bead on him and not
grieve that the battle has been reduced to many minor engagements.

Far channels come in the night. Wired beyond belief. *I* am a great nation
of dreamers. In, down, here, out, the earth. Plane noise going about the
houses makes for scale. Can you see this perfume? Everything that we call
destruction lies in the separation of elements. Thought is surrounded by
a hall. Sit down and take your feet off. You're training periods to dance. In
light of the words to this song, yes.

73

All Fours

load up in the sky
before doing a thing
shift gears in the ground
size hampering

perfectly awkward
dream sets are struck
making back pages
of a drive

I've got phone numbers
here to call
but no answers
to your many unspoken questions

off to boot
and repair to bank
a day goes
against the sound of ice

☐

man wants
name haunts
woman waits
old tales

extra lines
tell how

we breathe
together a plot

add size
to the measure
of a day
turned aside

sky tree
planes
vantage
proper number

☐

a fever states
obligations on tight
clamor for public
opinionated rainforest

conceivable light
half tone half balance
lights on glass
progression

☐

lanes converge on
habit of reflex
to jam the frequency
she walks to

75

the arterial manners
have neither a clue
to housing nor motor
sounds in all courtesy

fast strips
fan the bastard
as the ant
moves off screen

similar
seasons
little reason
to doubt

albeit wholesome
the name for advice
is silk
in a glass run

☐

cheers tear into the carpet
walls lean in
feelings well up
before noon

water returns to drop
form the top draw
flashes from a booth
on all saints' eve

rite cancels domino theory
sound has been alternately
cars going about the day
substitutions pennants on a line

☐

cavalier impresario
my beats are pressed
calling a halt
to splintered diction

two dots flash on
& off between flex &
affect
apart from bodily changes

what notes bang out
the bottom
are hot
but cooly handed over

decide to stay
in this realm
claim honor due you
sense data sent to you

plowing air back under
the trailer picks up
speed where the feature
left off laughing

□

size creates wonderful problems
space is the prize
coordination wins
by dint of the hit

□

cover me over
flip my lid
we came out
so you did

circles round a clearing
air doubles back
as a scarf
about the traffic

□

action is the property
of molecules
morning sun
my own

clear division
windows the day
water beads up
the screen

□

a graph of voices
would set them apart
from the turbulent feelings
they engender

thought takes
no time at all
words stick
on the page

in my head
between ears
and throat
for years on end

said again
differently
night after night
the way of life commits

bodies to memory
stray moves
turn out the light
clash harp

rope color
separate scenes coalesce
you'll feel it now
pleasantly

☐

the friends of sleep
assemble daily
to carve your
busy schedule

who was that
voices on the radio
turn indicator
blinks

around the horn
early explorers
pick up tips
get native smarts

salt
chips
beautiful
boats

☐

voice it out down there
this my office
ours
to slack off

awake a week
told it was up here

all along
the sky folds

☐

about to step
off the curb
and when all is said
something's left

undone
as if the words
were crying
from force

☐

approaching office windows
there is no discipline
shapes cut contain the real
a perfect match for space

focus beyond and
lights move motion
to the fore
in an array that speaks

Speaking Peoples

lime headlights. Curious Geo
on the coffee table in an
opportunity to share with you this
coagulant. Regular features
of a quiet night at home
installation. I'd like to
keeps falling back on
upstairs sleeping. I am
writing writhing. What are
is true? Threes in
as a trace, legend
on the face of a map.
negative on the street
and immediately stepped on
back in to order the extras.
A diary is selective and so is
kind of sound back of
I thought I told you to
TV circuitry, youngsters know so
still printed. Change the
subject enough, what's there to be
said takes shape, time and
time and a half. This is
voices say. Listen in on
coming from outside
times exotic nouns drawn
from a mental color chart
discarded by the philosopher.
Light sheds its skin and steps

down steps into water. Cracks
appear at pool bottom.
Breath, lights. Traffic at
palm trees below stretches out
the hills to the north, totally
dark. Curve in ceiling final.
pull-ups or sit-ups from parallel
didn't go. Could cut out as fast as
new pencil starts, some time in
Bay. Room pale sheets of thought
you'd probably object to
no, everyone very considerate
clue me in, solemnity, brouhaha
separated in banks. By the
order more checks and not account
day done up as a parody of sleep
humorist motorists stop to comment
remarks are litter. Potatoes, sliced

hireling losses trick you out
in suit to play off
the bank, old Hammersmith
Odeon venue by the black cab
puffs and dance totems
in the Crown Apartments
contender cowcatcher oleo
on account of the organic street
corner structure of our post-
pseudo-medieval lives looked out
from in pre-dawn gin
naps, targets, train on train
I did that a million

sounds dumb, but opening
the way for insertion of true
live particulars flexed in heat
of momentary delay. Stay tuned
as reception denser than tempo
ranges home looking angelic
cryptic is spelled for a break
in the act, exhaustion
filling up air with buoyancy
parallelism, cash, bonds
tomatoes, radishes, artichokes
thing express, expressly yours
as impressionable at this age
held under the breath, salutes
slippery straights & flushes
wit to wither, fade or concede
damage done don't doubt a dime
to stop on any way out won't square
the deal with the boys in back or no
you'll get by all right by not standing
tough guy talk a minute longer
than the door, revolving to
let out on town lines a certain flame
person, place or thing. Sharp points
prick the skin to keep design on
the face, myth on the mind, soul
on eyes, the way a state highway
holds down land, all the way along

half a block away. Timed
streets for days, zeroing
perhaps you'd like one of

not on your life,
I seem to remember you from
birds on a wire. The sun
is nowhere. That's awfully
let it soak. Time was
the elbow bent out over
the boardwalk, the beach
semi-gloss panty hose
up ahead here. J.J.'s
shaded by a row of olives
tilt the machine. The
surplus gets counted at
the end of the line, quarter.
What profits we make
we'll plow back in.
Being late makes millions
in interest for big insurance
scratch backers. Hold the
pneum-. Air keeps
stratoloungers, base periods
low profile ports of call
cities hanging coastal
by now. Beat the
close shave. Alvin
when we get down there
there's a fair chance
whether the weather
expectation inch or
slide trombone in an
oligopoly. As experience
more of the same, changes
imperceptible. The weight

dust blows off the top
cordoned off. Doubleknit

sings in the organloft
baldfaced placid banter
pointed remark zing terribly
bother you right now.
Golden slippers. I've a
snatch of tool you'll
third and gone. There
the lariat makes its grand
sweep, but who will
tighten, who be caught
the words get stuck
the referent locates the referee
attention drives the puck
a gap is. Jump
up a title in
your friendly neighborhood
missed much. While you were
water in the pipes
a daughter arrived at
events separated in space
had only a thought relation
temporizing. Tunes to date

august contemporaries. By the light
holding zones at cost, but the biggest factor
twilight of the zones. Then I watch
too bad we don't have
weightless. Instead of some
argument under the arms

play run it back.
Form in every inch of human
contract. Is there or
one way? Sealed. See
haberdasher for rock
through window. Past
claptraps phenomena
pulverizer swoon auction.
All right all right.
But the eaves, wings
holding the fall in place
time spent in viewing that
seems like a moment later.
Dog high pitch.
Time spent
seems like a thing. Illusion
rents object. Pays on
time, the horses' hooves
disappearing at the post
a thin band of air
collection agency. Parenthetical
fracture. This happens because
like that wouldn't you
anger hangar
see the difference. You don't?
shot his mouth off
so turned round in a dream
configuration. Satisfies
absolutely. In making a record
the sense of falling
(forward?) in space
then's transformed to read

presentation, but I
o bowl of sighs
you can't really go that
he's discovered the walls
they go along so far depending on how closely
you put your head up to the flat white surface of
and so on. But the only real
freeway traffic, buoy bells, rail yard wheeze & clank
terrific. And so I open my hand
and so do they. People
right down to when to do the
things like that every day
not at all bad.
particular sense of urgency
how things are. These are the

shake well. Your memory is nothing but a
don't want to stand in the way of
identifying with yourself so fully as to
number, size, color, an agreement
operation on the third floor. Somebody's got
light on down on the dock. Bump
smack into relation determined by money
heading down the tracks. The colors
afraid to let go of the rope, meaning
you live around here? Stopping
is a new line on carrying, minus
the invoice. Collect on all you've ever
here later. You'll know me by
hope. Calendar pages away, the day
'll hit the water in a different way
lives arrived at fire pricing

supernumerary as in a mob scene or spectacle
dictionary pratfall. Irma
Irma in a rush. Then I saw
moving across the surface
by minute intervals. The young
needs a tape to measure the
door to the wall, lines discovered
by blind bugs in baroque lighting
fixtures, sound the key to
erasing ten reams

self-contradiction the ultimate
invisible double. Legs
later shameful feelings
in tact. Blunt
statement would be ideal
holding pattern. In place of
time, a quantity of space
had been preserved in hill
form. Living in, up in the
sky mounts, the blood took
the black of polyvinyl.
Ages round a curb.
harboring. Take a reading
weather changes the dark
bridge lights where the door was.
Curve in and out of a bowl.
There's pressure on the pins.
standard footing. Back
in the sensorium. Irresponsible

I'm not going to bother much about
as one daily into the ground.
Water rushes before we start to edit.
Each point on a line's an
intersection. Drive a tract
the land's planted in different
big areas. I hear talk in
many places, all ways to arrive
are paper thin, perfect
bounce. Vote capillary. All action
the field can't be said to sit still.
I was framed. You is riding high
in sleep, folded into a peach
calendar. At cross purposes
an expanse of green meets the blue
of the sea sky, still grey from
totaling up numbers in a register

forge past valley. You don't say
stop giving things emotions. That's
the trouble nowadays, people are treated
when you're wrong because you see
anger in me. I don't think the difference
is important. No, she's talking about
what the dogs were after? Sound alone
is not enough. Film rhythm is in
the head. Chosen site. Lights go
stunning. A church bounces into view
the Olympics in L.A. next time. Why did
swimming alongside the windsurfers
forget a bag containing the complete
stationary pivot point is where I

got off and walked the rest of the way
in the snow. One's hair was long, another's
short enough to follow all the way
through. They put the paints away and
hung out to dry. Next week the shopping
craze will wear down the pavement in
vogue again, and a silver samurai belt
open seven days, will pull you by
the way you do the things you do do instead of
dwelling on certain gaps that might just
as well over half a million strong subscribe
to in off moments like the one this picture
fails to represent. Close to the face
the air is thin and fades a little
before the portico at dawn, a figure
concealed in the folds of this bathrobe
originally shipped to the director by
a story. But I could only think
even that. A flamingo and a lioness
days puffing vertical and horticultural
semblance. There the ordinary
which way to go. Voyages
discover a reflex. Time gone
over carefully to remove all. Then
again so we get kind of satisfied
there. Only ocean, three winds, sigh
minded him of a couch. The next room
was invented just in time to
banish intruders. He is not
a capitalist. She is not a fellow
traveler, the sentimental
color comes out of the earth. Sky

particularly rough on you. Easy
does it come apart by itself or
heartwood's durability, unless there's
cheers and racing about under bleachers
bugs in the grassy night, all heavy
sobs, rocks crack against the door
in time for walks from tracks
cornstalks, games in the middle of
a continent. While later on it turns out

entire strategies to L-beam rheostatic bite
on account of the behalf. When I was in
yak therapy you have to follow the whole
course. In the stretch, puddles have formed
breakfast, and we didn't want to be late
for hours on film, years cut down to minutes
in the auditorium. You have always
is located higher up. And on the roof
a door opens and a man walks out holding
"the football" seven steps behind. He
our president doesn't know where he is
in Brazil the evenings are just right for hard
work downtown. Jobs go to the first
strong man, boss or military miniskirt
built by Baldwin. I've been expressly avoiding
capital punishment. Beads are sweet
the oval wobbles along quite a bit
twenty-eight teeth and all so young
and she among them, laughing and kicking

how the west was lost. Not simply
framed frames piled high, torched, screams

from the balcony at every false start
this-could-be-it points delay
the inevitable. What was foretold
was recently promoted to the position of
given, wrestle with it. Subsidy
pink and golden over angularity. Where's
the courage to stand or, not simply, stroll
leaf beds, glaring promise off denial's
haughty triumvirate: steam, lesion,
co-nexus—plaid happens. Chest
heaves bales out over the platform
catch. Hope works ok. Size
flips over on its back
shape. Then cut it out and paste
the side of a barn somewhat between
Starved Rock and Newfound Gap
clouds half falling off the desk
conspiracy docudrama all around
says it. There's a thing or two
stew put up to simmer in a
Caribbean. Memory alters the present
hold the heat has on one's
conjecture as to granting
clemency, where one gets
high-handed lording it over one
night of a thousand days
chambers the sky forewent
argument into transparency. First
a wall with pushpins the size
red yellow white brown black
straits and seams dyed bright to
tuck it under. The sun is out.

Fine. So why sit turning
masking something you can't find?
Sure the other is out the door
being by for you and away as well.
Walls target proto-hypnotic eye span
as soon as a meaning wavers
lane violation in a rear view
two clocks back. But up and
inch by. And throw the coil or
stop erasing things, weed strains
without my attention locked putting a
tax on at the last minute
collapses in. The hold
dear to all land lovers
could turn inside out
liquid shirt. Streams
colored for sure the second
view of lakes and tiny
after day. Make
turns suffice to flesh
a golden state I've not
attained since. Flexing
champing at the bit
part to reveal major
form, arms and legs
moving off stage, rope
twisted tight as a
table top. Ow!
but the contemporaries
flew with the wind
an orange peel a
yellow blue-lined pad

what left fissures in the lives of the English
speaking peoples? Slowly they came
to discover the secret call of every creature
in the forest, the signature of each leaf
and stepped about on a plain of high grasses
where birds were. Above us the sun
follows perfectly, by force of habit. Years
a shell game. Low clouds part to reveal a grid
water in a coke bottle with sprinkler top
memory planted their feet in the dance
box step. Courtship parallels slope of roof
hair on the back of your neck. Song
praise plaint truth struggle hustle settlement
of all we've known. Notes stride in
the throat, walk with me. A clip-
on tie is wrought. Any city afterlife
can come south on the color, no.
Tunes on end, rhythm solves the puzzle, space
no product masters can conquer. Meaning thrives
this time, a lack bemoaned by those
who follow old scripts to the letter. Change is
upon the land and seas and over there on the rooftop
ventilator tops spin with the wind. Silver paint, rust
that pen ran out of ink, a bottle of pink
green leaves in the window. The boys went
across the street to the 7-11 to get a paper.
I'm floored, high up. Traffic in goods
but on certain streets all is not well. The cold
realize you have to take care of people.
Trees stand as examples to trees, shadows
To us, of our building on the opposite wall.
cat peaks around window corner, cars slide by

differences to get up and live to. Walk
switch habits, callbox, plaza. You lean
in and out of time. Lunch is already
a silhouette on the deserted court

take a look on the flip
side of thought, so called because
the garage was broken into. All four
panes thick with condensation
view of hills in the haze beyond
chilly out there. Mail that
upside downtown Manhattan. Fake cab talk
pieces the still. Head over there
could be. Parallels describe history
thick as postage. I've half a mind
cut rock right down to the quick
animal life, a trope the palms share
eye in the center on a chain. On and
clips in a desk work one on
empire and earth is. What left
silence is pre-condition and then there's
being. Those things shuttle, cook or go
new ore lens brook Lyn ease
to prove a point about time. Dispatch
clamoring in both wings. Plates on stage
serve as future. Between the actors
lies, total suspense, locked in by script
would happen. A double-headed
thus twice tongued and sighted snake
or none at all. Pouring, gesturing
made signals things, rain comes
into it, but we are no longer there, had

been enabled, would be having to catch a go.
Stops are disparate as sweaters
out of any in a station. Along wires
being very quiet, before sitting down to
show me how to make those hell of neat corners

of an evening. Discomfort is the first sign
up and take action, a swathe of light
mere illness. A glow, a shield, a belt
the approach to the airport, but he
all I can think of is the way
a narrowing process, but conversely
hips set sail for centuries. Climb
how you may, the roots go out in all
send word. Back in Madrid, our
utensils set out for another morning
collaborate with me on this venture
Geneva. Clickety-clack. Loud volleys
clothed and parted and room for three
bedside tables, lamps, convertibles, recliners
we live between and among. High above
MacArthur Boulevard for the past six months
judge the bullet. The boyfriend denied
feather duster, not a sponge in sight
the woodpile out back, the crunch
have at times daunted. Spool rims
chemical syllogism or grown man
carving old haunts out of chance baffles
then I saw you coming down from the radiolariat

shadows what you might want to hear. Glancing brick
green delivery paling to open the sky for receipt

cuts down the ravine. You place clink and windows
on the rear image. Outside sound, hairy spikes
tires on the road complete with look up
offering her a ride. Streetlights in sunlight
a controlled intersection. These scratches on my
still bare trees bear scrutiny, year after
housing the sense organs. Soft air when
grey rails and rust, the hospital on the opposite
balloon released above it. Some wind
then a bug up close. These sails remind me to
give you the slip. Bird moves with
weight, feet, fields, weed, deals, great
height above and below. The universe is
added on. Each integer stands in an open
square, where we were to meet the sailor
how they live in cities versus a sudden wreck
stand around the cars in the middle of traffic
mosquitoes already. The hook pulls the stage
to the cleaners. Birth and motor grass has
hands that touch the edge of the counter
happening as well. A thin solvent is
really starting to get me. Appeal to appeal
bladed dirt. You have. Then start it. The guy
I saw twice today miles apart, once running
bike up hill. A sound is coming over

Autochthonous Redaction

AUTHORITY VESPERS

May try industrious lapping at lakeside. Old habit at a glance, but the punctilious rails glean rye. All I've ever envisaged careens floorboardward in an imagination of tiles. Try to pry information off the fuselage, push raw metal endeavor tied to a post. Tangled organs were Gorky's parking spot. There's air outside an idea, more space than meets the eye. The pull is furious, flag snap in storm. All along the warm interior of the mouth houses resource. The elevated crash diction completes the image sentence. But behind that these interpolations can never get, the base slides noiselessly under foot, buildings heave into view, and an accelerated procedure takes up the slacks and drapes them over a chair.

HIGHLIGHTS OF AGREEMENT

Home fast onto the useless tract Corinthian panoply, whole anterior sweeps counter the impedance, sway. I've been all four prepositions and intend to lay about, counting curriculi and billeted at the mouth of a second story yarn spool, twirling at least every whip of the way. Then the sound of a passing car. Around is how we are brought by the phenomenal world. Not the one you read about or is it? And when is or was that? Philosophy may be ridiculous for a grown man. The book, the orange, the cube, entryways curl up in the water. Communicating arrowheads stand for rapid movements in the history of supervision.

EDITED BY HAND

The irreversible line of sight levees a tariff on words. We don't understand the green leafings to be here after. What song goes down with a ship, nearer my odd "to be", farther than even "sure"? Hazard lights mark the night. The tables turn slowly, about one revolution per lifetime. Salt spray. "I saw the brain. It's like an ocean."

A HAND IN TIME

What we'd kept saying, that all would be well, just as we'd begun to be not believing, became true on the seventh day. The rest had done its good and what's done's curved upwards, pleasing that "that woman seems to be perplexed. . . ."—the television, no bother really, rather a reality check (uncharacteristically), the window—daylight. Waves of relief in relief against a sea of trouble, this we can make out, and do. To contain the thing is to be free, at ease at last. Times place, places time the voice, airs out the window air out the proud boast, design thinking, industry at the wheel. Along about now the hands folded, flexed, press on. The stars are out.

BIRDS IN STONE

Up and down and in and outside no front or back. Pulling this way. Speed locked in. Dried out space the smallest concern a reversal. All day night. Confusion pouring through a point.

INTENSIVE PURPOSES

A man in the future wishes I could see something he sees. The land scraped and pushed by wind and water far below, ice long ago. "I haven't been there for years." Machine gun laugh. Take the trays off so she can go. One sympathetic, one indifferent face. Red mustache curled above the jaw, snow fields below. Drinks followed by tears. Cloud cover moving to our rear, sun up ahead. Adjust all you will, the planet will continue to roll, eastward, as if backwards, disengaged. The frontier press plants one foot down to earth.

SUPINE BLENDS

The way California stretches out from the past you could head for the door to all stimuli and not spend seven years before the blast. Acres stream against the pilings, car horns sound at dusk, pink over and above the bay, one moon and a star maintain purchase on particular blue. Lights spank the eye. Cheerful laughter sounds at mid-belly. A guy yells, "Mike!" or something, out in imminent night.

ABRUPT TONIC

The first madman had large round hair and was waving his arm. I locked the keys in the car. The newspaper depicting a face through glass lowered then before a charming one in person. Afterwards, and there usually is one, I listened to the stories of the tribe, turning from one to the next in motivated light. I saw the score, then the delayed broadcast. Leader coursed through the gate. These angles on boxes are lit at night.

COLOR NEGATIVE

He stepped into the corridor and shook hands with the third man. I . . . but then . . . I . . . A whirl of effects displayed itself, gratuitous. Often a few planks would become dislodged. But the cycle of events placed him outside ordinary considerations, he thought. Likewise, doors opening inwards as well as outwards accommodated a constant succession of arrivals and departures daily. Nails interested him. He found a rusty tack in the bottom of his sandal. He reflected on its manufacture and conceivable age, flipping it into the ashstand. The other man had given the building ten years. Not the structure, but the business of what went on in it. The sky was pale orange and violet. The sky was grey. Puddles beaded the wet-mop lining the rooftop. Wind blew white clouds into blue sky. He did not bother to look. He glanced out the window—sun on brick wall. That night he heard fireworks. A corner of building jutted into the sky. A green lamp not turned on made the same shape, upside down.

EFFLUVIAL VERSIONS

Wind distributes the leaves. Writing copies speech. Copies are distributed. The constituents waver in the wind. Storms "nearly wrecked my father's house / just quartering a tree." Talk pages leaves of grass. Mind you walk all the way around your object, circumspect, hearty, and quick. Draw bow from quiver, then draw box containing dots, label and forget. A confusion of flowers bursts into shirt. Astride a mount, the cattle man mosies into the margin. An index pages a stand of trees.

DATA PRESERVE

A line of trees sways me. Marooned, camouflaged atomists flank the delegation. Have you signed? Wake to include service happy numbers, the vested interest mounting to pi. Hercules steps down. Hermione Gingold in black and white behind turquoise beads, ice afloat Manhattanwise the men in ties stand just outside. That door swings both meet and depart colonizes abortive breathing stays. All's utter. How pasted-up the rain remains and glances back over cloud issues. That man's belt is still. The women in the far corner have discovered a tiny contingent in the slight membrane connecting aerial contract with leaden weather. Blind by vertical Venusian blind, a transparently fraudulent rendition proposes mounting stasis over a hill. Swirling, that's why Jones can't talk. Smith can't hear right now. Would you move that plant into the light? Or isn't there enough power? Slowly up the stairs comes one part of the picture after another smokey carbon.

DIGITAL RAIN

Damned if you do, darned and dirty in the fifties, that negligee air parts
sideways so it's only a walk-through. Over and over the shoulder multiples
shudder in classified dossier light. Chips plink on a raised surface. Phones
go off every several second thoughts. The work extends, it is extended, the
operators play out the line, their line of work extends to leisure horizons,
providing jobs for natives of the future and futures for naive operants in
a code ruled by link of hand. Traffic counters are installed at intervals.
The bridges fairly hum. Some stain of fellow guard refers to rail in careful
attention getting device mixed up with blood. Shoulders square with
estimated flight path for the spring. Claims hover to leeward. We're coming
about. Bush detectives check in at the old colonial residence hall, shadows
under mere hats. The effect of costs is bent double. Screens read leaves.
Waiting for callbacks scratches the file on suspense, barely audible and true
to lust status, more and more light on hold.

Seventh Street

Over and above
old captains' houses
now fallen into
funk, the train

passes. Further, trucks
docked to load
manifest ramps, then
darkness of tunnel

and the passengers reflect
on each other.
Light nicks the
surface of the

globe, even under
water. This lazy
description of the
way things are

tells more than
it knows. Say
something about conditions
and you have

that to look
at too. Your
station stop is
this writing's end.

Stutterstep

To put an end to
to consummate
and deliberately
go on to the next

this will to close
pulls the rope
taut
tightens the knot.

At ease on
the way to
morning, evening stops

to brush a
few drops
off "See you later."

Lilacs set a
beautiful boundary
between yards.

A red six-
sided figure
about says it.

But then there's
more road
and changing tires.

Oh patiently do
the rains lie
under the ground

until the rockrose
comes white petals
fresh each day.

Tense
unlocatably abstracted
a man walks out of

a door
and onto the street.

Habitude.
U-turn.
Crescent wrench.

I would see
through the cracks
in time
a can of paint
upside down on
the globe
and a boy seated
on a hanging
scaffold
grins cheerfully.

Then I would
go off and
do something else.

The end repels
as it attracts
the life of
an initial mind
for lack of
a better world.

Hold something steady
you are shaking.

Go on then.

Archangel

Air arcs overhead.
Light gets in
through rectangular holes.
Imagine customs reduced
to a bite-sized
grid. Locked into
habit, the daily
passengers drive the
self to work
for more craziness
in industry. Foreign
shores tremble in
light of great
heat. Beef sources
are more obscure
than any writing.

I'm sitting here
watching this chair-back
revolve behind a
desk. I'm sitting
here thinking just
how otherwise to
conduct my affairs.
I'm superficially repeating
patterns from memory
onto the wallpaper
that is this
world. Across the

gulf, a mess
of flowered bodies
lies past aching.
The insulation I
feel is made
of money and
the ability to
control lives. I'm
simply put. But
I can wrinkle.

Voices delight in
sporadic dislocations,
touching
the key points
on a map
of crudely rendered
deletions. Happy as
a baby tire
hugging the blacktop,
a man in
the neck of
a woods discloses
ties to a
woman in shoes
and a bright
idea, glad to
be out of
luck and onto
the main drag
where work clocks
the body for

seed and life
hangs by an
arm of the
sky. Talk covers
the tracks made
of every bed
ever slept in.

In my solitude
I have occasion
to get to
know a lot
of great people.
We clown around
in an arbitrary
way for about
two thousand years.
Then it's time
to get back
to work. Refreshed
and invigorated, we
plunge headlong into
an increasingly complex
series of problems.
There's no way
we're going to
finish in time.
But it's ok.
The machine that
keeps track of
all this is
out of order.

Curved air, high
windows, heavy traffic,
light industry, foreign
investment, local suffering:
color by numbers.
Something that one
ought to do
or must do
is an office.
The camera pans
a drifting fragment
of the flat
thin ice that
forms in bays
along the shore.
Complete days reach
harmonic proportions, narrowly
entering the flood.

Ice Cubes

then
begin
over
and

sleep
to
control
costs

no
overhead
no
inventory

but
dreams
count
you

among
the
players
in

the
all
universe
commodities

sweepstakes
where
futures
rise

and
fall
breathing
normally

□

by
doing
something
I

could
figure
in
nature

□

why
do
you
identify

car
color

as
yours

see
thing
think
uh-huh

when
any
other
sign

might
occupy
your
mind

close
tantamount
slender
fix

  ☐

effervestibule
notation
sensation
when

at
the

hearth
of

new
life
on
earth

we
can
see
everything

as
mass
potential
(for

Carla
Barry
and
Asa

☐

these
thoughts
are
too

rich
for

my
blood

these
feelings
too
much

for
thinking
to
clutch

☐

motorcade
cops
on
bikes

cars
limos
flags
mounted

on
hood
support
camera

it
must

be
the

President
on
the
streets

of
San
Francisco
as

we
go
play
ball

at
the
Olympic
Club

☐

close
but
not
quite

your
note

said
it

was
Mondale
last
night

at
the
Saint
Francis

☐

the
hiring
of
professional

criminals
for
selective
jobs

we
can
do
that

get
them

to
stop

copying
me
we
can

do
that
get
me

a
show
in
Minsk

we
can
do
that

□

I
don't
feel
like

working
today

I
said

first
thing
this
morning

now
bleary
after
dark

I
hasten
to
add

you
never
can
tell

but
hazard
a
guess

step
out
into
air

□

fantastic
sadness
humor
or

fierce
scrutiny
of
what

comes
by
the
stars

arc
in
the
sky

□

you're
good
at
conversation

it's
like

walking
you

put
one
word
in

front
of
the
other

□

arms
race
a
rush

of
power
to
the

limbs
build
more
or

be
poor

military
Keynes

of
no
small
means

I
wonder
if
I'm

kidding
myself
about
pills

till
down
will
come

kid
crib
and
all

☐

the
dead

hand
of

the
past
falls
gradually

a
fund
of
knowledge

a
land
of
numbskulls

a
maximum
security
person

☐

voices
at
lunch
time

air
flows
across
the

vacant
work
stations
hum

"American
Opinion"
a
storefront

on
San
Pablo
Avenue

now
completely
empty
inside

☐

brain
salad
alphabet
soup

Dagwood
sandwich
and
a

piece
of
cake
then

Mr.
and
Mrs.
Potato

Head
inflate
and
support

the
soft
underbelly
of

the
bloody
banking
business

⬜

screams
from
the
street

at
night
aren't
at

all
unusual
we
won't

always
live
here
I

didn't
have
anything
prepared

⬜

each
numbered

hour
possesses

two
faces
seconds
none

scaled
senses
of
the

money
time
coming
undone

☐

thank
you
for
calling

to
dull
novelty's
intensity

a
journalist

must
be

a
human
shock
absorber

fime
but
we
better

be
prepared
to
pull

all
reference
to
the

future
at
any
moment

☐

sounds
close

the
hatch

heat
smacks
a
shed

light
on
data
poses

the
instantly
soluble
fish

☐

in
a
room
(world)

full
of
people
(history)

I
wanted

air
(poetry)

hit
the
street
(Chinatown)

cut
the
concrete
(subvocalization)

□

water
hammers
white
blossoms

green
leaves
pressed
to

the
window
light
reflected

in
above

the
writing

hand
makes
evident
tremble

□

these
cubes
designed
to

cool
your
drink
dissolve

faster
than
sound
thinking

□

behind
the
wheel
before

the
screen
before
the

mast
behind
the
eightball

between
takes
not
really

doing
much
of
anything

☐

greenling
sheer
Black-and-tan
Hopkins

propagation
shadoof
inanimate
raison

exodontia
Lawrence
avoidance
Turks

feather
restorable
inamorata
perdu

☐

I
am
not
what

I
used
to
be

belly
to
the
ground

in
so
many
words

□

tender
ministrations
of
delay

wrapped
attention
clogged
shocks

□

plus
she's
friendly
red

rabbit
upwardly
mobile
home

□

he
had
them
eating

out
of
his
head

☐

waking
to
wash
up

heat
water
for
tea

get
some
work
done

rain
comes
down
roof

☐

icons
windows

pop-up
menus

and
mouse
support
all

closely
simulate
the
Mac

☐

fantasy
performances
hillside
remedy

Alfred
Stieglitz
speaker
glass

tobacco
cozening
capitalist
idea

☐

print
maroon
on
grey

each
letter
stands
out

bottle
green
under
sepia

veins
mix
your
world

☐

dark
sheet
blind
double

claw
hammer

giant
clam

foreign
legion
windy
city

my
dog
has
fleurs-de-lis

☐

pre
Ohio
tortilla
a

concise
if
meager
formula

for
what
there
is

left
in

the
refrigerator

□

the
lariat
describes
an

excitable
rialto
in
air

theater
of
laughing
operations

ribbon
development
rhythm
bath

□

a
dream
rage
built

on
clouded
habit
stuns

the
world
with
rich

frontal
determination
one
man

absent
alone
owning
everything

□

dry
scratches
on
the

surface
of
the
moon

over
my
shoulder
blades

heat
lightning
in
an

East
Texas
basement
window

☐

we
have
combined
the

dog
and
pony
show

ended
early
caught
bus

ridge
electric
eye
shadow

ladies
sweaters
half
off

☐

wrapped
in
a
clock

sleep
music
continuous
waves

holding
pattern
in
place

hide
and
go
seek

who
is
that
other

I
dreamed
of
waking

from Covers

Kerouac narrating Pull My Daisy. A dead spot —nothing to say —exhaustion.
Long pause. Then he starts a low mumble, hesitant, labored, unclear, from which
he deliberately, gradually begins again to build a spontaneous commentary on
the action —a group of people stranded in "an old kitchen apartment in eternity."

in planning a picture
I like to leave one side open
to my friends

she must be out there
by the canal or
on her bike somewhere

we used to look like freaks
to the other supposedly normal
people wanting to be left alone

imagine how surprised
we were to discover a
contradiction between

going on as ones
and holding hands
being called Mom and Dad

the mouth goes on
arriving at a station
of colored trains

I'm performing an improvisation, following Steve Benson. In my piece, I read shifting grains of white powder behind my watch face, which represent stars. My speech comes as if from a group of extraterrestrials coming (back) to earth. Concentrated clusters of star powder translate into intense, compact verbal runs. Eventually, the pace slows down; the words are fewer and further between. When I stop there's applause. I'm elated, hope the performance was recorded on tape.

> reading these words
> realizing the potential
> striking a balance
>
> in time
> to have sex
> and maybe take in a movie
>
> to have sex
> an anomaly
> in the working order of things

Larry Price reads a work consisting of long words read extremely fast. The reading accelerates until separate words are indistinct, then the voice blurs into a solid, clicking drone. I'm aware how this performance mystifies some members of the audience, but I enjoy it.

> enclosed in a system
> of wires leading out
> toward more wires
>
> in a powerful ruckus
> Ahni is
> directing the whole thing

with the help of
a medieval chorus
crowded into the hall

chanting the
one same song
sitting late still

With two other nameless characters, I'm highjacking a dark blue pickup truck. Stash bag in back & jump in (others ride in cab). I'm wearing a navy watch cap pulled down over my head as far as possible (it's cold) plus a small black top hat on top and white rimmed glasses. View of self from side.

I meet Miles Davis sitting on steps outside a music hall. Strike up a conversation. He's friendly. Takes out his teeth at one point. Has real teeth underneath. I compare his situation, waiting alone for a gig, to mine as a poet, dependent on hosts, though the audiences are smaller of course, in my case.

"You've played Albert Hall, Lincoln Center, right?" I ask Miles if he knows the other players signed up for the tournament (now it's tennis).

"Better than they know me," he responds slyly.

what of it?
no ordinance
had been passed

by any body
saying she had
to *be* the road

Francie is working on a remarkable set of paintings: portraits in a heroic mode, the central image a woman of massive proportion and smooth, rounded surfaces, fully integrated into a background including children and animals. Francie's husband helps with the painting, doing detail work, and her son practices filling in a figure with brightly painted curlicues. He'll be an artist himself some day with this kind of training.

Ericka has also created a work of art, a form with a central stick contained in or braced against an oval support, like a belt buckle or a barrette, which she has titled, wittily, "I'd Walk a Mile for a Thistle."

I walk with light grey paint sticking to my shoes, grey suede hushpuppies I won't be able to wear to work any more.

> figure and ground
> supply the eyes
> having eaten from a garden
>
> and giving away likenesses
> the artists greeted
> me heartily
>
> on my way back
> to fix a fence
> my confidence restored

Norman Fischer holds the attention of the group. As he breathes, he mumbles strings of words under his breath. At length, phrases emerge. Some are bemused, but I explain that Norman is merely demonstrating a fact of life—that we are subject to a continuous flow of language, that it courses through us, and that we can tap into it at any time, that experience is like this. The key point is that no increment of language/thought remains in place, each is contingent and transient, in flux.

the road to the palace
is lined with pre-arrangement
we stop for a coke

this scene dissolves
into abstraction painted
big as life

the details are vague
the picture is fuzzy
the words have been erased

Lip Service

"Nice dress"

               (irony canceled
               into transparency)

means "fine body"

               hair & eyes notwithstanding.

The date rolls around.
The pressure lets up.
The heart seems boundless, rapt in whipcord.
               The glare . . .

   Openendedness gives you the pip.

Cross-reference that back to parent company Britain

        and I had an idea once
        ending and offering up alternations
        in an ensual

(suites, rollaway, crib, etc.)

             bound & determined

  I'm sure

         to bottom feed
         not at random but

waiting for "CALL COMPLETE" . . .

        with a penchant.

The stopwatch stitches the field of vision
to the lifetime guarantee.
This is the first shot in a long salvo
of simple, neat solutions
that are wrong.

    Blow ye winds / all over / the Kingston Trio . . .

There's an oh in my soup.
It's a transverse wave
perpendicular to the direction
of my advance.
A device for hurling clay pigeons in the air
Inclines westward and upward
Toward three replaceable atoms—
A situation involving the love of two persons
For one of the opposite sex:
An informal "secret shopper."
A few scattered elements
Pick up the pace.

        A bit stands in for a vague trace.

      Body confidential
      Logo nova
      State zenith
      Basic specifications for all major types

A mysterious solution to a mysterious problem:

If the reader now pulls on the rope, a creak and squeal inside the box is
heard as a foot or so of rope comes out.

But are we willing to admit that an enormous building full of ropes and pulleys could be just as smart as we are?

Warner Clements of Beverly Hills, Calif., disliked the wraparound dismemberment of his worms.

First Thing

It is important to do something meaningless

"Meaningless" here might appear in quotes were it not an undifferentiated part of an unexamined expression. Thus there is an unconscious judgment as to what is meaningful & what is not. In fact, the "meaningless" move, the one *outside* the structure of the game (in this case, the job) may be the most significant, or productive, or meaningful in terms of *another* game (for instance, writing) (or simply relaxing, getting one's bearings, fording the gulf between sleep and work).

Enervated limbs

Nearing toward late afternoon

A declivity

in order to cut expenses
we will take your time
and give it to Ken

this narrow definition
of where things come from
is neither humorous nor false

Hal & Poco
Norm & Dave
Marion, Pepper, Edgar & Stosh

Vic wants to talk to Ken on Monday
"We want to keep them out of the operations,"
he wants to say
                (meaning the Board)

I am slow, phlegmatic

                        3 peacocks strut by
They just say nothing

                at the end
                too romantic for words
                of our collective practice

                thoroughgoing investigations
                versus
                a distillation

                of the day
                are displayed
                "artificially"

                the elements
                media barrage
                . into the public

Leaves stand outside this business environment

What is a note? The smallest written thing, a mark
for a sound

If I scratch my day in sand on the back of time
between sips and a passing cloud

the forest people

                alternate in an impression

of sticks

        What sticks
        in the mind
        like thunder
        is an impersonation
        backing into an elephant

This quick & brittle-hinged claptrap
My unguilty
The rest has slipped away

        Real & right to be torn up
        Actual processional temporal place

at the end
of the day
the elements

of our collective practice
are displayed
"artificially"

thoroughgoing investigations
into the public
media barrage

versus
a distillation
too romantic for words

A Mental Finding

The world
        and all its burden of traps, dishes,
        forget-me-nots, wheels, ampules,
        laughter, freight, comets, deals,
        parentheses, batches, cloisters, fair
        havens, place settings, ground cloths,
        pollsters, minions, theories, lecterns,
        rings, criteria, sorts, and all manner of
        blistering palms

was found by the side of the road
                        lacking
only a local node.
        Efforts to resuscitate
        the dead have ended
        often in a backwards
        representation of the day.

The personalities, the ambience, the montage, the sound
all these graced his mind in a trice
but *what happened*—this escaped him. . . .

        The sky opened
        on a possible life
        the senses set in relief.

        Bearing in mind and reversing
        the immediate past has long since
        become second nature, a habit
        built up to the status of I.D.

I doubt it.

       The strand
       The bullet-proof vest
       The carbon copy
       All attitudes of a world I can only . . .

connect the dots.

       That's what I was trying to tell you.

The missing element
recedes from the point of view.
Light drains from the day—
that is the nature of evening.
The first one of summer is a metaphor
for freehand, a writing written in script.

Going away from it
the weight program
I have broken into it
broken it into pieces
about the size and shape
of blows
about the head
not about but away from
anything fits this loose place
skimming the surface
of dreams
set up during the day
collapsed at night
distanced, positioned, reduced
a May weight removed
to let June have its way with it
a delimiter totaling none
of schedules

drawn into the scheme of things
delicate, nodding, half diminished
there in the milk of a syllable
the perfect fret
caught in the forgotten sentence.

These heady plans chase sound into a bush.

Flatten the letter!

A spoon
stirs
shadows
"I'm over here"
up in the time zone.

The cymbidium
tends
toward the grey light
the other side
of the wall.

The other side
of my head
is your head.

You have
a hat on.
The world

barely fits
under the polar
ice cap.

I have more plans
rolled up
in an attic locker

than you can
shake rattle and
stick to the subject:

a speech that wavers,
a language
that takes hold.

The president never explicitly authorizes covert action
but signals his approval by means of a mental finding.
The public never officially acknowledges this betrayal
but indicates its mortification by way of a spiritual loss.
The person never actually notices the repetitious layering
of experience but circles the planet with a red pencil
to convey "error."

The date

        June 4, 1989

        Remember the Beijing Massacre

        &

        Long Live the Students

The way the world has
of reversal

        The power of absorption
        The power of brutal repression

(rewrite this later)

Scared teenagers with automatic weapons

The jagged edges are smoothed over
to proffer a picture
                    when rhetoric fills the news

The world picture source has fashioned another banter
The forgotten palaver of indigents creases the air

Lines roll down the cathode ray cheek of the party chairman
Picture a less complicated version of this unwitting career

The weather station
The golf cart
The maze

                    A man sings
                    what he has been singing for 20 years

what
have
you
been

dreaming
 lately

          building
          the
          body
          out

of
effort
takes
the

mind
off
the
hook

this
world
comprises
an

assemblage
of
brief
sessions

there
is
no
other

but

it

is

incomplete

Pacific Street

Words, such as they are,
come to mind only
in the instant,
however banked or consigned.
The whole sway of color,
latitude, echo, stricture,
lust is compacted
and dispensed
in a bare mention.
The series of parallels
collapses into a solid wave.
The skew lines animate
slight gaps in the waking
text. There aren't margins
wide enough to force the gram
into place. The place spills
over into the hour. The weather
charts a combination
of greens and blurs.
Landscape is matter of fact.
The risk stretches it.

Two empty white plastic buckets
are dropped from the roof.
Plastic sheets flap from a scaffolding.
"Not on my dress, on my clothes,"
a woman's voice protests
good naturedly. How much
can you tell, hearing or

telling all, about the way
the day aligns its weight,
skaters and beach for legs?
I don't put any middle parts
in my rhyme,
I only end off
And blurt. I blab a line
there and paste it in here.
The motor scratches at
the windows of a deal.

A Pattern Language

Although the lists appear arbitrary, in fact they are highly ordered by the particular modes of their arrangement. For instance, watch, game, friend. My friend gave me a watch, which I subsequently lost at a game. I went back to find it, and it was still there. But the narrative twist is gratuitous. Story, legend, book. The associations are more than assumed. They are the lineaments of a gratified desire.

The botched job
The list
The amphitheater
The sight of blood
The abandoned station
The pair of gloves
The articles of war
Some silly old fool
The serious interest
The hank of hair
The plenary session
The gross margin
The bolt
A reduced, clarified experience
But I bore you
The effortless grace
The new
The abstract
The belief in original sin
Parataxis
The formula-one race car
My one good pair of cuffs

The day laborer
The hitch
The satisfaction guarantee
The backwards flip
The bat
The least common denominator
The wash
The very slow ballad
The gentle breathing motion
The wax
The end of side two

Caught in this net of things, we tend to sort as we go, listing into the wind.

Speedball

I am reading about Speedball, a futuristic arena sports game where players use cunning, courage and strength to bribe officials, tackle opponents and hurl a metal ball around a dangerous steel arena.

Just then, the bed begins to tip and slide onto the floor, which has filled with water.

At this point the dirty work was done. We pulled up the vertical suspension cables in a few days, we fished them up with tackle from the pontoons down below, and it was like catching eels, but these eels weighed about a ton and a half each.

The IRMALAN SDLC Gateway 2 is a kit containing hardware and software that enables a personal computer on a LAN to emulate an IBM 3274 or 3276 control unit giving workstation PCs on the LAN access to an IBM SNA host via modem over switched or leased lines.

Is that a sentence or are you just happy to see me?

The emotional climate varies with the geocultural terrain.

In Pleasanton, the emblematic beast is a small round potato bug with armadillo-like ridges on its humped back that skitters across the sidewalks at random, distant intervals the way sporadic traffic appears on the mostly vacant four-lane divided boulevards, as here and there jaywalkers dart across to avoid the poorly timed lights of the excessively controlled intersections.

We travel through the zones, lassitudinous and hyper by turns.

What a night! You've been abducted by two thugs from Chicago, knocked senseless—and now you wake up in a bathroom of a cheap Las Vegas hotel. If you don't come up with 100,000 big ones in the next seven days, you may be trying on a pair of cement shoes. What could be worse?

This press release!

The potato bug had found its way inside.

Whirring away, an emotional disturbance rocked the otherwise placid sentence. It's a life sentence. I forgot to mention it to you.

The gratuitous is so unacceptable to most people. Who do they think they are? Only within the parameters of a game can rules be said to be violated.

One wishes to tear away the fabric of the personal agenda, the other imposes a heavy burden of numerous mild complaints. One accepts the world as it is and sets in motion an elaborate armature of perceptual alterations. The other sets about to change it.

I first read of yogurt in an Ian Fleming book. It seemed arcane, European. Now it's in every strip mall—"ice cream without guilt."

I first read of yogurt in every strip mall. Now it's an arcane, European "ice cream without guilt" in an Ian Fleming book.

There's no way I'm going to rewrite this to anyone's ultimate satisfaction.

The mythic, literary referents of modernism have given way before the onslaught of contemporary information. It's something we're going to have to live with, not knowing "it all." This goes in the book called "Thought"— the one labeled green, for hope.

That's an ancient and medieval idea.

These are only states of mind. "Down in the dirt." I have only to say what's on my mind now. But there is no now, only a succession of retrospective regards approaching identicality. This list goes on and on, a token of my affectation. The overall pattern is drenched.

The world is big with currency, filters the values through locks, open to word of mouth. The test is a series of tricks trapped out as production and silently slid through the morning break. Each worker remembers the tools from the job before.

Time's concentric banks pool up in the jam jar facade. A list of visions sways the crowded elevator, but the singularity of common experience bolts the business down, and there is only one floor, the second.

That Joy persists informs her every waking move.

Dayparts

for Ilya Kutik

1

Wrists, trees
mysteries of poetics—
it's impossible to translate
so much of what goes on
in your churning oceans
belching skies, etc.
of a mother tongue
and still seem to communicate
from a human skull.
I found these letters
in a river basin.
The landscape enters a contested ground
in sleep—wide as these bare plans.

2

Large world with churches,
obelisks, and Basque Finns in shades—
this no-nonsense altitude
fills the proscenium
with castaways, halting only
to pick up speed, starting early
to protect the rhythm at last.

3

The motion detector enters the poem
by way of the sentence, sensitive
to a fault. Loud lines
cross back of no personality—
an idiosyncratic pitch—
deft at libel, historic
when mysteriously dull.
We get stuck in a meaning jam
on our way home from work.

4

"Talk about what one should do
as if one could do anything
instead of only what one can do," he thought,
"strikes me as absurd."
Later, filling out forms, he thinks,
"You are only too happy to cooperate."

5

Since last I wrote the master vampire of Rumania
is no more, a stake in the future
put through his poisoned heart.
And 25 unutterably handsome
American boys have passed away
to remove our man in Panama.
Fresh air blasts across Eastern Europe
and in Washington, the same stench.
Shift to drug wars, now on TV.

6

The limits of a buoyant will
make themselves up
as it goes along.
There's a chronic float.
You have only
so many choices—
therein lies your freedom.
You could get hit
by a truck any day;
that's how it's enforced.
A vague, big number
of reasons add up to naught:
you live as you will the life of a radical surd.

7

The life of a radical surd:
you live as you will;
reasons add up to naught,
a vague, big number.
That's how it's enforced,
by a truck any day.
You could get hit—
therein lies your freedom.
So many choices
you have . . . only
there's a chronic float.
As it goes along
they make themselves up:
the limits of a buoyant will.

8

I keep trying to get back to those parts,
leaves hanging off stone eaves and shutters
claiming the world for sound, but a mysterious
dog pulls my steps, and the accurate representation
is the one broken to bits on the wheel of time.

9

In California, spring and fall
occur at the same time,
in January.
The leaves drop to the ground
and branches put out
green shoots.
Grass grows on the sides of hills.
Rain, better late than never,
prods the seasons on.
Prose sorts them.

10

The live east west corridors
open to non-stop bargain
turrets in sync
at a variable margin.
Image this, the rhetoric
of an earthly blow. Times,
then the one off the past.
Nothing any more interesting
will be happening at the next
street corner, intersection, or

nearly running up steps,
fatalism breathing as dice.
World powers salute a bare
token of the breath a mere
walk took out of you.
There are ways, and the red
day is bland with desk drawers.
A winter grin comes in
fast, muzzles the monotony,
stones throw from emphatic
lessening. Talk is of hand;
the buttons do or don't line up.
Present this card at the window
dated narrow, await, stranded
on the hour. Conditions relate,
that's the fact that brought us here.
A dash left most of our
other considerations out.

11

In teasers for Bud Bowl II
we have attained a new level
of iconic reflexivity:
an ad for an ad,
a rhyme for a "truth."

12

Aubrey's Nameless Examples

13

That joy exists—
this is the further consideration
these words urge.

14

Fecund sadness
beaming in shorts, flowers,
soup if the power
wears off. A will of
its own design, spreading
the fingers of a lake.
There desire lays down
to rest. Across
and into the trees.
It was not to be.
You've had it.

15

A slow, backward spiral
downward into despair
reverses itself, an occasion
cut by the height of the sun.
Sudden release into childhood—
exhilarated, pedaling fast.
The open ticket, the dime
novel, the abandoned lot:
there is a lot of change
in this brisk, splintered transmission.

16

The most vacant hour's the one
in which most can be found
to be most unexpectedly done.
Rates of exchange, burdened
designations, pie charts, eyes
locked into sets, a chain
of beings wends its way
to the door, aloof, but
implicated in the campaign
speeches of another decade.
The accordion accommodates
a note or two of a dirge-
like waltz in the un-
distinguished foyer. A
passenger thinks, "I have
to get off." The stain
improves with division.
A boxed set of anecdotes
pitches the loveliest retreat.
The lack of meaning or
emotion or intention with
which such sessions commence
only serves to enrich and
enliven the possibility that
some event, heretofore inconceivable, may
carry the day past its moorings
into another particularity of sense.
This time it's set
to go off in a dark
surcharge. *Tempus Fujitsu.*

17

After yesterday's papers
have been put in the bin,
we'll see what kind
of shape we're in.
Bits and pieces,
a tissue of lies,
I have no truck
and am fully vested.

18

"Take out the earthquake."

19

A record of peaks
and troughs written
in sleep protects
private parts, projects
intimate avenues, available
shortly before dawn.
The sentence argues
for a more manageable
workload, lanes diving
down hillsides, characters
stood at attention.
Days broken down into
increments afford the sponsor
opportunities to reach
a target audience, depending.

Open the hour, a
tradition since six a.m.
A flower has more
separable parts.

20

The vocabulary of advertising
played in silence
against the chord of news
provides a gentle background
humor for the breaking
into parts of a personal
day's work, miles
from the time being.
The integral students
find a place
in the scheme of things
by cleaving
to the absolute
the way a baseball
cleaves to air
brightly
and with the fist in it.
These rhetorical templates
left us by the ancients
have been spruced up
by the boys on Madison Avenue
now exploded worldwide
so there is really very little
we can't say
or so it seems.

I keep trying to pry
the letters off the wall.
It does exist; there are
boundaries even words
can't leap across.

21

Cumulus, Mandela, Valentine,
Marciulionis, empty, clotted,
similar, sinister, unbeknownst,
caprice, rivet hockey, planetoid,
quid pro quo, cantilever, requisite, fox.
It's late in the millennium.
The forms are out of date.
Write somebody a postcard.
I sent a fax.

22

America hurtles forward
in an insane frenzy of efficiency
subdividing time to an iota
at tremendous cost
as if, by Zeno, by brilliantly
organizing everything we could
amass time itself
against the tolling of the century.
Against this hygienic mania
lies the unraveling:
space; words recorded in sleep.
A feather brushes

a surface in the mirror
a hand reaches through
to barely figure.
Days go transparent in
the relief of stairs.

23
Relaxed and well
I wrote of today
a claim I hope
you can make as well
reading this.
The subjective states
what the objective leaves
unsaid. It feels right
to be living
in a community prosody state.
Artistry baffles
the conjunctions.
Most of us simply
report for work.
Leaves dazzle
that hang from the branches.
Trees are our principle
mental comfort.

24
After the difficulties
of correct spelling, serial
murder, and extravagant

gestures inappropriate to
any context, the prospect
of a simple, straightforward
communication possesses
a disarming appeal.
That flight, however,
is booked, and we are
forced to go by ground,
wending as we make
up our way. In this
way, we actually discover
more to say, although half
of it gets lost in translation.
Finding places to stop
and rest can be
the best achievement of
an ordinary day
an occasion fit
to be tied up
by a redoubling
of every effort
until the moment spills over
and it's time to get back
to luck. Late arrivals form
the basis of a new
century, part figment, part
chill, a situation no one
could have predicted.

Rushes the Sun Parts Daily

"Without strict controls we would have chaos."

Days harbor empty rooms, turning about an axis. The ant's day's a complex
of twirls, incremental leafy tenderness in the up-to-the-minute aside.
Around my thumb, the paper swells with detail—there are mentions even a
spokesperson wouldn't make. The decline of mixed messages into the soapy
west—it is this that disappoints the key grip with a hard-earned voucher.
I deliver the goods and collect the bads. "Are you a perfume wearer?" An
unfamiliar, but pretty woman appears 'out of nowhere.' "We're doing a
promotion," and the insect world is doing fine. Then the sky is not simply
cut out of that ridge the way a paper branch might be subtracted from the
rest. I don't know substantially more now than I did twenty years ago. In an
Econoline van. The country would have come apart at the seams but it is
compressed. The light does that, moving the earth around in front of it like
an interesting party. You are dying to return, to go back to where you began,
to retrace your path and make of this series of separations a contained
whole. You are living to exceed that reduction, to place an emphasis on
the new part that doesn't yet fit, to outstrip the comic pace in part and
breathe through the air in your chest. A swift delight catapults the lifetime
membership into the blank. We have a way with this, this unspecified
nature, faltering, short of definition, and in our umbrage, a marvelous
compassion resides.

"If we make a mistake, we make it twenty-five million times."

I have an outdoor workstation I utilize from time to time. Here I twist the
rhetoric of persuasion back on itself. This is an alert. The call to action is
immediate and inherent; it requires nothing further, but implies possible
worlds. Let me dispel one misconception. There is one world—that's the

news. Future worlds are multiple, as possibility, but reality will be one. I confess: the limits of this life are choking me. But what would be better? "You can't be free unless you have a context to be free in, that's what we're seeing now." Here in the sun and chain-link noon I muse. Sick of routine assignments turning me into a funnel for backlogged to-do's, glad only that such an expression 'sounds like something else.' Nothing could be further from the truth. It's the possibility of seeing from the outside that keeps me sane, if anything. That useless 'something else' an air I can move through, an artifice I can really use. So I take my place at the margins of central practice. You've heard us say this before, but believe me, I am not crying wolf. If bitterness creeps in, or an arid irony, it's not me, it's only the interface I hurry to confront. "My spirit longs to be free." How naive, and yet how true! Here a man sits with his self-pity, in shirt and tie, a harried middle manager with nothing for the moment to do, at parking lot picnic table, under a summer sun. The wind stirs the leaves. Plaintive, but sound, I'm of a mind, bound to head back in. An arbitrary scheme might force the unsaid. Expressions latent in production, unnecessary by-products of normal operations, these are my inchstones, indicating a way out. We have staked a lot on this program. Now we must perform.

"If the landscape changed, we would have to change."

The Central American gardener uses a vacuum to remove leaves from the parking strip, the small gas motor mounted on his back. He wears all green. All detail is eligible for all time. The back of my hand is a reservoir. A guy drives by in a "bitchin Camaro." Such facts, like the wind between buildings, are the background static of our industrial strength. From these foundations are our very figures derived. I await the programmatic forays of others, then ride them to the time of their lives. Instant ambition documents the paltry burlesque. Who's to say what's worthy, anyway? Maybe a clerical worker whose men have gotten violently fucked up on drugs. But there is a pattern. The secretaries dress so nice in high heels and nylons, with their hair done and a different dress or suit every day. And their boyfriends pull up in Camaros wearing cut-off T-shirts and hightops and tractor hats. Point is, the lowest rungs on the corporate ladder are occupied mostly by young women. The office gets increasingly masculine as you move up. And the equivalent baseline jobs for men are in the warehouse. Identity cleaves to the allotted space. Gravity feeds on pallet jacks and bar codes the lot. A man could get lost down there. A charismatic, slow-moving homeboy, with his goatee and suave manners and big trunk. I once saw him chug down a half a bottle of tequila in post-season on-the-company blow-out at Castro Valley pizza parlor. That was his last season with the team. They said he'd once been a good athlete, but that year he only came in off the bench and usually turned the ball over trying to do something fancy. One thing though, he never gave a shit. Used to show up for games sometimes in later seasons and grin from the bleachers, sharing a little joke with the world, it seemed.

"We are bombarded every day by people's attempts to convince us of something."

We must therefore learn to analyze arguments logically and develop our own powers of persuasion. But who is this "we" so easily invoked? The wind wraps the building in swirls. Voices percolate. Words carry their own weight, as well as that of the entire latter half of the current century and thousand calendar years. Laughter has. There aren't any places to stop in it, so history removes time from experience. We were cautioned about that, but forgot. As one pundit put it, "I'd rather stay home and stack beebees." And in the interim, a margin opens onto the dead of Neptune. A dad drives a wagon away. There is a succession of trailings off, each subsiding gently into the medium. To chat is bland, to ululate sublime. I had a hack license back then. Lean your bulk and mass into the prevailing text and you'll make out the light of day, gone rapid in an extensive list. But the waves aren't

there, they only seem to spill over the rail. Upright, cantilevered
furlongs carom against the montage. Perhaps Darwin Tu expressed it
best when he said, "I better not believe in too much, I'm confused enough
already." An enraged skepticism braces itself for the Fall semester. Leaves
harden and curl. The harvest is in. It looks good. This land belongs to you
in me.

"She has no idea what our lives are like."

A slow day at work. Radio show on the common cold—the usual poop. I
feel one coming on. Tender passages. Hot & sour soup. "No MSG" = MSG.
Approaching University & San Pablo one dreadlocked wino hails me from
afar—"Hey, Lurch . . ." "Lurch!?" I grin, & he laughs, realizing his mistake.
I give him *Ice Cubes*. He says, "Hey, it took you 12 years to write this poem."
Dates for "Oleo" have been misprinted, 1975 for 1985. Cindy bends over,
arranging some boxes for Margaret. Vince comes up behind her and starts
to gyrate his pelvis. Cindy looks around and says, "Do you want me to bark
like a dog?" Black eye from foul by sheriff. Turned away again at "The Dead."
Charles clears brush. A day: "not enough." After dinner walk to hillside
view of city, stars. Later to Caesar's for drinks and dancing. See Fausto in
his white wedding suit & silver tie—on the prowl. No work. Exhausted,
angry. Sore thumb. Fitful sleep. Burr haircut. Haircut feedback sensation.
Rainy day. "We *are* the food!" Wake from dream of Vineyard to bright blue
sky with white clouds just like in dream. Sleep in car at noon. To American
Soil for six bags of general landscaping fill. North, Poindexter, Secord, &
Hakim indicted. Reagan sends 82nd Airborne & 7th Infantry to Honduras.
Pull kukuia grass runners from along side of house. Solstice. Double forfeit
at Canyon. Press check in Albany. Read Ron's book *What*. Miss Kevin
Killian's play *That*.

"Let the weather be salt in the gradual system to be."

Let the weather be food for the gradual rating bazaar. The mix of meals is a cause worth branding for duty. Let the hands ray. Let sailors preside in places best spoken in parts. Oceans open the letter sound by sound. The weather shines. Let continual nations confide. There is no border we cannot delete or cross. Let subplots interlace in an embarrassment of contrivance. Simplicity is extraneous. It's a complication. Let grammar strike its bargain and go home. We say as much in the manner of our physical leanings. Let the jocks be funny and let the freaks grow strong. Let the apartment beautify the farm. Let wives press steals from between the times. Every citizen is entitled to a place to squat. Let originals be lost. The lineage of versions is eternal. Let harmony wax the boardwalk. The songlines cover the map. Let the hand let go of the throttle. Let the brakemen look decent in the dawn light. Let the factory air subside. The toxic waste dump stands next to the nature company stands next to the house. Let each stream go unencumbered to the watershed. Let it rain, let it piss, let it jam. This now tomorrow is another different day. Let all the old familiar places come to be. Go back where they came from. Let the pearls of wisdom roll scattered on the chilling floor. Let invention abound. Let the young mechanic in the provinces outwit the aged bureaucrat at the capital. Something there is is a birthright in the head. Let a hundred schools of though flutter. Let the body house the spirit in a building before long. Let the mind entertain its client states. Let the vacillations begin.

from Counter Meditation

1

Slow down
and the insects catch up with you.
Slow down even more
and they fly right past you
mistaking you for a wooden stump.

3

Two people kiss,
go off together.

What happens next
is on them.

6

Between a rock
and a soft spot
unity
and virtual fragmentation

the United States Postal Service
Commemorative Stamp Club
makes its presence felt
on the eclectic American plain.

7

If all words
were blown away,
which words
would be the first
to recur?

Does what's said
grow like a sprout
from silent earth?
Or is it a belt
in a moving assembly
of words?

"yes"
"hot"
"way"

Slowly at first
building a house to last
corners cut
in the ongoing course of events

the way I figure
and the way interruptions collide
the body turns over
sleep startles the owner
in time to wake with all things.

8

You have completely mastered everything. Now what!?

10

I got one of your moons today.
The space behind it whitened and went out.

These words occurred to me
somewhere in Helsinki.
They seemed to come from you.

I showed them to you
and you said you might take them back,
to which I agreed, absentmindedly.

16

I've been in Jimmy & Lucy's House of K,
and I've read in the Red Hall,
and now here I am
on Sol Uhuru's Art Shack.

But wherever I am
I'm not entirely there
because I have to leave room
for this.

18

The form of all lands
is formlessness—in all worlds
there only exists verbal expression,
and verbal expression has no basis in facts.
Furthermore, facts have no basis in words.
All worlds are silent.
All the teachings add nothing.

Names, rounds, Americans,
citizens, troops, taxes, makers,
lawyers, headlines, concepts,
years, reports, votes, companies,
prices, users, concerns, bankruptcies—
the nature of all phenomena is uncreated.

The open doorway
of a plain brick building front
through which the interior walls
have poured down the stairs
and out into a huge pile
of rubble on the street.

A photograph of the sun.

19

Eve off.
As in, "We get Christmas Eve off."

21

The limitations of
a brown notebook
are three inches

by five inches
by a person
unable to escape

from a shadow
of fluctuating dimensions
even in a hundred thousand million eternities.

23

That one knows and is
only desire
deconstructs the problem
of being a person

so that the elements
of living are laid out
across a plane transversed
by waking solids

no negatives
no bleeds
no color
no discounts for multiples.

24

Delusions are inexhaustible.
I vow to *enter* them!

The huge sand-strewn esplanade
The mostly empty parking lot
A few flakes of snow ...

While you were out
Some vague details
ate your lunch.

28

There is nothing
to write about.

Rain once
in a long while,
intense assignment
followed by free fall,
the personal dissolve.

When you close the book
the wet ink prints
backwards
on the opposite page
a desiccated Semitic script
illegible by half.

When you wander through
those ruins stand

for whatever you pick up
on the back of your mind
pressed against doorways
whose walls are no longer
leaning in
under a steady barrage of dead signs.

The night sky
is terrible.
Periods
can't be distinguished
from noise.

38
Why this obsessive need
to record? Why this
going back over? This
reduction of transient, ephemeral
lived experience to marks
on page, tape, or
disk to be pored
over from every imaginable
angle later? Repeatedly?

"Once you hear the
music, it's gone in
the air . . . you can
never capture it again."

Balance Sheet

Pieced lines and lined pieces lead to the blind shed, its light
green finish peeled off before the eyes can catch hold. Stasis
has become a way to get the job done, an unlikely reminder
blessed with the virtues inherent in a peach pit, part of something
much longer, but remaining, for the time being, a cradle to stillness.

Falling then into an imitation of sleep, the western writer
dreams of spurs, cactus, and Comanche trails still fresh
in his imagination, he being a man of no small ends and
having a surplus bond with nature. It seems so simple
that even a foreign parliament could vote on it without translating

its parameters into an equivalent juvenile stream, the worst
of it being over, the first a quick glance to the left
of center. Progress seals its own fate when getting down with
a debenture or two, and the only way around it is to fake
a rhythm into the rectilinear booster for half an age.

Then the ornamental report falls due. A mix angles into view
while cherry blossoms come down on either side, and the nether
world coughs jargon up into the fan. The history lesson
collapses into giggles, because there really isn't any way
of determining what led to this impasse, only an alignment

tending to grace the weather, a particle haven, a spit
on which to roast the occasion, for all the good it will do.
The same ideas that jam the machine, however, also dislodge
the letters that were waiting to be delivered, and they go off
like so many three-minute eggs, off white, soft, precise

enough to answer the same damn question that called up
those ideas in the first place. There is a mild swivel
about the day, a forest of cramps backlogged in an interruption.
There is, in fact, very little to be done, and even less
time in which to do it, as the diving evenings draw near.

At one end of an area, it's foggy and cool, with a hint
of sadness in the minds scattered about the pale, quiescent
avenues, while at the other end the sun, great author
of an engrossing, superlative pulp, sears the grass in trapezoidal
patches, bakes metal to a crisp, and wears soap operas down

in the health clubs instead of barely thinking. Aghast
is how the intervening country pays its due. The wealth
towers over the examples. Such needless display compounds
the already laughing matter with stays, pins, hardhats, joints,
and bricks, a mild form of nuance reversed into a bent, counter-
       punching

ardor that leans and will not go away, even when daunted
or put up to ripen in an unassuming, persnickety obsolescence.
Much later, having survived the near miss, not to mention the prosaic
slide presentation, the acolyte reaches home full of surprises
not so much to others as to himself, embarrassments such as giving

the steak to the cats, ranting over a limp, being a bear
in a rest area, impossibly, trashing the scene. He follows
the sex pixels. He follows, and it follows, in his career.
That is the straight map. Verbatim. Heaven hasn't the time
to refute it. String these marbles far from the blasting

lamps, the power has hold, and only old caverns resound
in a constant, the bought, coherent simple. Why not?

Let them drink clear water. The rain is in the air but never
comes down in summer, only heightens the air with a long
glance, perfect for spotting the drops in barometric pressure.

The music was being recorded so he didn't need to listen.
Full measure of bathing days reclined against the will.
He held in his hands the print of a former time. The sun
flickered through tense, a wayward strain to be anything like
the same. The fields were wide, but he cottoned to them.

Time can start again now. Instead of all these words
and no place to go. Only now does it help to have a plan
so that you know what you are supposed to do next
more or less. Things change from year to year but the sky
changes from day to day and stays the same from year

to year as far as we know. One wave comes after another.
Each is different, so they're unpredictable, real,
unique events, but at the same time there is a very
reassuring sense of security in the constancy of their assault
as if from an infinite energy source, in human terms, like the sun.

Like a volcanic eruption that releases tensions built up over
eons inside the earth and wreaks havoc in the daily lives
of fish and men, coughing slough and ash across the sun
in an awful revision of all that has come before, so an
interruption in the text, straight from the realm of reality,

where visions and versions clash by the light of a windward
moon and relations break down into fits and sobs and
defensive maneuvers aimed at gaining a toehold on history,
must, by the rules of this separation, be elided, folded
back into the continuance, a kind of stay of judgment

195

enabling a reader, later, only the vaguest clue that the
whole convulsive, withering, strident, referential mass didn't
spring into being in just the same rhythmic, variable
sittings as that later architect, you, reader, convened
to see what was up in a day. The interruption that is

places bets against the interruption that isn't. One
should always think and say that being is, but at times
the wind comes heavily down upon the racket. That noise
made retrospectively down the street signs its name in
chance, the wayward, confluent stamina it takes

to hold a job. In place, the time is only an instance
the parcel of land addressed as we. Parallel that back
to radio segments lost in a clamor of bricks. It takes
a unit to know the rules. Cane hobbles weep, the we
in an altered you subscribes to time. I've said everything

we hoped or planned in terms only they would understand.
Metering lights. Quality fools breathe style on the sore
points. I wouldn't want to have that camerooned.
An exquisite sensibility is worse than a row of cans,
useless as fame without money, a tidy, clinging kind

of self-satisfaction. Give me piles of used appliances
drenched in the crib. The noise of my earlier paradigms salutes
my need to know. There's a roll bar on the toll road, a song
breaks into the house, finishing off the last of it. You have odds
but the elegant works have an ache for all I know, being held

down by my otherwise perfectly assumable dental mortgage.
It is neither weight nor weightlessness that defines our host
but a continual referring back, a conversion of flux

to facticity, that language we thought you might find unsuited.
A calendar dotted with tire irons just floated a loan.

Newspaper articles, fancy dress, articles of war
and of law, these tones are merely parts of speech
in a syntax whose nouns are the times we set to sea
or made iced tea, filed insurance claims, or sat
on the porch feeling nice. The or a breeze ruffles the sheets

pinned to the line. They move over into it. The sun
carefully fills out a form, leaving the address blank.
Nowhere about this natural world is human drama, only
the integuments of the soil, washed out, splattered
into thin air, a combustion deprived of sound.

Snowshoe Thompson just went by. Chicago's Boso
with a big piece of turf in his helmet holds the ball
aloft. Boulders dot the embarrassment, dead trees
lie cracked and broken over the back pages, torrents
thrive on an orderly morning toilet. John C. Fremont didn't

write this. The fishing party collapsed on the point
of completing its catch—it hadn't wanted to end
things that way, but there you were. In any case, by breathing
we would certainly hand in our résumé on time, and it was only
a little way to the footbridge we had been told about

more than once. Then wetting our fingers at the breakwater,
we figured white would be ok for the exterior, clipping
our heads to the garbage cans made out of plastic. It was a pleasure
being left for dead, because no one would ever again tell us
we had to be somewhere. Instead we would always remember

the unfinished portrait of George Washington hanging in the front
of the classroom. A chimney stands where blackened
rubble covers the ground, an end to fear, where before
a sense of what might happen poisoned the neck and back
as viewers craned to see, as clear as mud, the ridge bum.

Wan rain, the slamming of blankets, then clarity
as stars stood straight up above the dampness. Way west
of this characteristic a movie was being made, waving glimpses
in the anterior cruciate night. Stars had gathered, the paper
come. A western woman took it in. Good morning to all you witches,

ghosts, hobgoblins, and especially all you skulls. Nothing is
        "instead of"
anything else—everything is itself, separate. That's not why
so much time passes while I don't write these words,
words that only serve to elide the Gargantuan truth of detail
waiting in the wings of a prayer, prayer that is this life, words

expressing our paucity or excessive force, one, an echo of that
voice I'd thought to hear then all but gave back, seemingly,
into the ground. Players, teams, Lithuanians, why should I
like anything? The legal staffing of batches wrenches
the sound you rub up against, making your friend come clean.

Doing things slowly, deliberately, takes up the better part
of the morning, one year. The work that is slowed, ongoing,
stays a mass of crystal with its slime. An incremental burgeon:
chained to a wall for five years, then: "We apologize for capturing
        you.
We see now that holding hostages serves no useful purpose."
        Released.

I'd thought to say something else, then bivouacked
and charted the rest in gold. My pulses were only
going to repeat themselves anyway, up to a point, as part
of the synoptic breadth. Land rays channeled to tunes,
a birthing, crested aromatic, semblance included. Tossed

a ball or something with some guys. There is no 'place'
for women in these networks; the door to the apartment house
is left half opened. Everybody needs to have some kind
of a help desk. These things don't run by themselves,
quite the opposite. All right. I've got four boxes

and I'm going to walk through each one. 1. Make
hard cuts to the opposite block. 2. Always jump stop
to receive a pass. 3. Execute the required move and score
quickly. 4. Rebound and throw a hard outlet to the wing.
Squeak squeak sound of rubber soles on varnished pine.

As if the abstracted sense impression were a kind of bottom line.
Are these miracles science or are they just marketing ploys?
A whole rote sequence is packed into battery color.
The thickness of days, a clip art, subsidy, parental care,
and all that lucky time crowd into view. It's standing

room only in the bleached-out segments bearing little or no
resemblance but bringing chills to the table, as leaves
are used to make a lithograph. Perhaps I can help you,
but then again . . . How much goes by in a minute, how
little in years! The clamoring, roseate substance of which

a day is made straddles the intervals, calm in a winter factory.
It falters like a headache under aspirin. After meditation,

cut a finger slicing bread or quarrel with someone you love.
The accompanying psychic shock will jar you out
from the docking station to which you have become hopelessly

affixed. Day rents space in a word. My watch
is going south. Honey is sugar; avoid it. The object
is replaced by a panoramic: "The World of Objects."
I don't *object* to that, it's just that. . . . Regional
differences pack the house. There is no mass experience

only that of individual beings. The mass is a facade.
White sugar all over the freeway. Behind the palisades
a bumpkin Dionysianism has set it. The illusion of being
kept up-to-date fades as you stand before the black painting.
You have to wait for your own retinal imagery to disappear

before you can see into it, the luminous mix of reds,
greens, blues, and blacks forming crosses, H's, and squares:
all black. It is a discipline to see. No sight but that
which uses art. The far station a mix, the landing
pads coherent in a further study. I wouldn't put it past

the answering impulse to swear up and down on a stack
and cast aspersions up like smack, a piece of man that works
and presses the button in time to topple the credenza. In case
there's no floor, the pathway leads to a mention, the particles
pile up into a body, rested but still slightly sore in the hip.

Morning, and a surround of nations stymies you. It sounded
ok in your head, but when you say it it sounds dumb. Wood
duck stamps for your bills and a no-parking space labeled LOADING
DUCK: before and after lunchtime treats on the second-to-last
day of not just any year, a line through these points points up.

Your excessive response is much appreciated in the quiet canyons
an undifferentiated economic impasse makes manifest, just
above the airline industry, several levels below Kansas City,
Missouri. I dance from pixilated candy that you have picked up
on the colorized situation to our left, where reality seems

to be running out of ink. Freud's Taos stands in for
the phrase. If something very important is being repressed or
denied, home values will soar. People in the late 40s, early 50s
in places like Carmel, Santa Monica, Cambridge, Greenwich
   Village, and Majorca
de Palma will gyrate to what you said. It will take a certain type

of person to piece together these bones. They form an instrument,
but I have taken the precaution of removing it from their sight.
The problems are not insoluble, but each solution seems
to present a new problem, so that one's work is never done.
Typing HELP followed by the name of a command displays help

for that command. Explaining how to get through a pick,
I believe. Triads are powerful crime groups with roots
in ancient China. *Rouge et noir* is a game in which
rows of cards are dealt and players may bet on which row
will have a count nearer 31 or on the color of the cards.

Does every game have as its object to win? I don't think so.
Home rhymes part fast. Stitch it here, along the grain. An
emptying out of old rules spreads the attention all
over, prepositional to a fault, as well as nowhere, that non-
location so precisely current as to limit every step of the cliché.

I would like to summon a few platitudes as we speed
across the plateau: something there is about the first-person plural

that does not love us as well as we believe we know. The middle
        part
of anything gets lost in a forest of beginnings and ends
which meet periodically, only having extension by virtue of veering
        off

into absentia. Bank, Ron, ball, Bowl. An extension
cord, a VCR, an antenna, and eight articles crammed
for an exam. Whole earth. Half sky. Wing nut. Dress lunch.
And in sleep, laid out beneath a police grid, dodging sex
dreams and trips to the PX, lost in a pulse, the same one

that ached in Uncle John's band, there, compliments of California
Casualty, the wayward instance flees, racked by theory,
fluorescent in haste, looking at five years, as it undoes its
splendor in advance of the road, cataloging a split in the nasty
ventilated cosmology recently employed on a part-time basis.

Yesterday I slipped out of the groove, and today had a good
deal of trouble getting back in. It was as if I was on the outside
looking in. But at the end of the day, the paper hit the front
steps the same way it always did, or would have anyway.
I don't conclude anything from this, on the contrary,

it doesn't seem to help much at all. The moot wings
of political roughage tear away, and we can see who's lying
on the fork in the road, throwing money up in the air like words
and endearing himself to no one in particular, a crude, vagrant
saunterer in correspondence with the stars, although their order

has never been more irresolute, because a hash mark has suddenly
planted itself between the earnings of an enervated public

and the only reason to come out here in the first place:
to shoot turkeys! Birds like turkeys and eagles are used
as metaphors for winners and losers in an attitude of mind

as American as apples to oranges, I mean, you can't really compare
what's lost to what's been happily gained then can you? It's
wise to be hopeful, grateful, and thoughtful, though not always
          possible.
Up? Down? Up down? What mood have you designated
to plot the morning shade? This is what you were

trying to tell them, that it had become impossible for you
to simply be one person. So that whereas the other focused
almost obsessively on a narrow range of social phenomena,
          attacking
it again and again from various angles in a broken, idiosyncratic
syntax, you enveloped all manner of disparate evidence

in a kind of emotional who-got-what-report, input,
processed, and published under the congenially rippling
banner of a commercially historicized rhetoric. Tough
totals. The anger flashed from pan to pan. Then a zoom
would be in order. I'll roil before two bits dent insight.

You have to gape at a flock like that, all birds pale
before the evening whirl. Going back over it in the second
half of life, you know barely more than the first time—
only to recognize it, the impulse pointing south, or west.
An aggregation of fragments, this life represents an opportunity to
          sit down

behind closed doors in a quiet room and concentrate on one thing:

House of Wrecks. A novel idea is what I just saw on the freeway
and how it works into my current thought stream, barely and with
             the edges
still visible if removed at some distance, say, a furlong. For as long as
this cautious adumbration hulks over the development cycle,
             research will have

to be speeded up, although we have no funds to spare for it or even
             to speak of.
And speaking of wrecks that speed into view for the first time,
what characteristic, when slapped with a fine spray, matches our
             synthetic
order in half the splendor? A plot to correspond with haste?
No, I don't think you mean that. It's just something

you put together in a moment off. An otherwise endless tunnel
of thought breaks out into the open at the written word, finite,
particular, breakneck, given to common usage, bright with age.
The wind is yea long. Our life continues without our knowledge
under everything of which we are most haltingly aware. The news

is last on our list. The taste of all that is missing most flagrantly
catches our style. Habits converge, and a lamp stand totters
in the swirl an eddy rudders under time. Run the numbers once
again and you'll find a split infinite call, a conglomerated put,
and a wholesome diffidence in the face of world capital, when only

yesterday your best bet seemed to be to construct a light vessel
and pour yourself into the reading, alight with what to do
about the alarming mass of billing currently accruing but wise
to the off chance a senior analyst might show up to sort it
all out. Now the answer is up for grabs, not that the question has

exactly been put forward, it's more like a bemused look on
the furrowed collective brow of a beta test group, or an illness we
        read about
and immediately begin to imagine we have, or a flowering tree
        whose name,
if only we could remember it, would break open that awful aphasia
from which we have been suffering ever since, ever since what?

Our birth? Or a simple metaphor, if metaphors can be said
to be simple, that would explain our position, speeding effortlessly
two inches above the glass, and not break into a million pieces
when held up to the light of philological scrutiny, a history
best left open for another time. The garden is covered

with a rich, fine carpet of spray. The ocean must be nearby.
A man born in the middle of a vast continent marries a woman
born on the coast of a small island. Their son, your correspondent,
born near a lake in the middle of the vast continent, situates
on the far edge, internalizes the vast distances the land mass
        manufactures,

rolls down the window on the tides, and, after a protracted youth,
        rolls up
his sleeves and settles down to business, doing detail work on
        contemporary
reversible conveyances. Behind an able man there are always other
        vegetable men.
In America today, the mainstream has dwindled to a pathetic
strand of calcified imagery holding the mind in thrall, and the
        margins are fat

with unlikeliness. Weeks go by between sentences, is that what's
        new

about them? Remember that variety is an important characteristic
of the power aisle. Include combinations of large and small items.
Make sure the signage faces the front entrance. Avoid randomly
          placed
stacks or displays. Line everything up in neat, even rows. These
          cautionary

trails have been beaten into the bush, and we follow them, not
          because
we believe them to be leading anywhere in particular but because
          they offer
paths of least resistance into the interior, which generally turns out
          to be
someone else's exterior, but that's another story, stopping only to
          pick
the burrs from our socks. At rude angles with the way with words

the next blurt may be your own. There will, at all, be no surcease.
Into every other particular segment is injected a lifetime supply
of space, feeling tone rounding the character bends, false
witness creating a havoc of secular miles. Rage and shame enjoy
charter member status in the dormer pantheon we wear on our

way to work. It's a happy tab and a brisk summer tantalization
to which we have pulled ourselves up like zinc, and miles to go
before I wake. If I have taste, it is only for stuns. A story
line is a jail of bedposts. I have been meaning to write in poetry of its
own necessity: an opening. In our configuration centers, we can configure

a thousand kits per day. Line up and be counted I always say.
Five words after those words, we find the word "words." This
is a statement of surplus value. Any value implies a surplus.

                All hands
direct. These doors, torn from the jaws of time management,
open to porous copy on a litmus roll. See how vast and wide

the world is! Countless universes, known and unknown,
                step through
your minute concern. Why do you put on your seven-piece body
                at the sound
of the pound sign? Because Great Action, herself, appears, to hasten
you on your way. How long will it be before another entry graces
this gate? I cannot say, but stay up high and lean into the querulous
                light

the morning stars propose, bent on recognition, thriving on a tiff,
dug into alternate means, fledgling, where a band convenes a sound,
color-coded, reimbursable, just, festooned, and slick. I got a
                long-term
disability brochure today; that's about it. Moon resident in pink
                clouds
jet moves below overhead, you peel back the light on little kids
                on the street,

their sound I mean. That torch of hers. I started walking across the
                star-spangled
war-chest drayage under night's flip visage, not interested in
                anything I might
find, just out for a stroll, minding my own business really, though if
                the truth
were told I had none, for it was with no particular purpose that I set
                out, other
than the hygienic, wholly negative one of clearing the decks, so to speak.

What's different? The stars are gone. Day lies pitched like a hammer
in its cradle. Already the substitutions have begun. New York's
been going down since '88 and San Francisco has been rising.
Rain banks off rooftop water tanks, fog pillows on a dry bay.
To be a risk manager in a party dress, what's better than that?

What's happening? The line of roles stacks up to be a complete
                 bypass,
a way around the main event, slipshod if at all extent, humus
black, flung attributes in the net of all seeing. I've got houses
in my lobes and they're all open, doors and windows spread
                 to the four
winds. My foot is nailed to a shrine incineration. "Guess who's
                 coming

to dinner." "A ghost." Having outlived body and mind the raging
spirit yanks a bulletin board from the wall, speaks in the night,
softly, incomprehensibly, no tape machine, no phone, three or four
hundred dollars extra to smoke on a sailing expedition with my
boss's boss's boss, whose home, burning in the hills, he'll never

see again. A squad broke into the RCA buildings, abandoned
and sealed up for two generations. They went down into the cellar
                 arcades,
crumbling museums of the retail stores of centuries past. They
                 located
the ancient elevator shafts and dropped through them into the
                 subcellars
filled with electric installations, heat plants and refrigeration
                 systems.

They went down into the sump cellars, waist deep in water from
                 streams

of prehistoric Manhattan Island, streams that still flowed beneath
        the streets
that covered them. The sense of a city is war. The exhilaration
        mounts
in cooling plants in the outlying areas, a chorus to solo monotone
invoice tracking, a budget aside in a maximum battery

hairpin, resisting historic aphasia for horizontal reasons
if only from the legs on up. I guess the syntax that prepares
these lies lies open to any of us; we fill it with our various personal
chambers of horror, fitted out to wreck our sleep, images flat
against the rippling rhythm in defense of which we step out

of line, curve around back of the convalescent hospital, pick up
broken glass in one hand and check out every brick with the other,
secretly laughing on account of the compulsory overtime. If it
seems a random, solitary course, it is nonetheless one we share
who have nothing but the space under our feet, the salt

in our wounds, the baffling whispers from out in a bright hall,
and the miraculous streams of signals to wake us in time
for the workday. I have a feeling that no amount of preparation,
no matter how thorough, will be adequate to the moment, wherein
everything takes place. And yet it does not exist, except in

anticipation or retrospect. Thus meditations on time must end
in paradox, followed by taking the conversation off line. It is the
        brilliant
shortcoming of words to be inadequate, in the ultimate, to any
        subject,
and their savage grace to always be able to change it.
Life goes on, we always say, but does it? And so what if it does?

I won't be mollified by a panacea, er, a placebo, I'll sue the bejesus
out of the file server, I'm not complaining but I will be damned
and fry in hell before I totally accept this, this completely
              unacceptable
situation. The discharge in such a system is colorless. It empties
itself and the person goes on intermittently, deflecting annual
              epithets

rather than placing too much emphasis on particular nouns.
That's when I cram down my business-as-usual hat. But
the cost of goods sold must be factored into the equestrian
rattling the air with sword and shield. A sound or ache
is a framing device. In the foreground, pain. Inside the frame,

freedom. The fact is, and it's unfortunate, that before one has
had a chance to fully understand the situation, one dies.
The only conclusion I can draw from this is that one must act
on incomplete information. A certain level of attainment must be
              eschewed
in favor of cursory fact-checking and a quick trip to the loop

to pick up socks. Mine were knocked off by your insistent,
              paradigmatic
pulse, the life of style aflame in an extra inning, the wages garnered,
the heating lamps tilted back, all manner of what-have-you
              spattered and
crossed. And there, if I can just take this phone call, you have it,
              and it's
worth something, but only briefly. You'd do best to plow it back in.

Any such summing up is followed by a wide trough, like the silence
that follows responses to questions provoked by the posting of year-
              end results.

There is a dip in the blather quotient, a period of days during which
attention, although not unreflective, fails to nail itself down
        scriptwise
whether because it is simply too diverted by the ongoing rush of
        detail posing

as daily life or due to a kind of digital reticence, an unwillingness
        to sit
down, open the notebook, and begin, clueless as to what might
        transpire
there on the page containing the marks of already eclipsed
        sensations,
whether mental or rotten, curious, half-hearted or gut. If we do not write
it is because we are out there selling, pounding the roads, renting

cabins by torrential mountain streams that carry us off in our sleep
while we attend sleep school, unaware of the coincidence. Comedic
errands tug us across the changes. We are not ready to borrow
        another motor
until the music changes. Then the music ended and we were treated
        to the
clear rainwater sound. It had been what he had imagined the world

to be, streets, people in cars, windows, what others would later call
the common things of daily life, as opposed to what, metaphysics?
That was the first sentence of a work called "Sadness." But it had
        actually
been hammered out in glee, the type smacking the flat-skinned page
        in time
whose fluid beginnings housed torched chords in the rock hole wax
        in shifts

et cetera et cetera until there weren't any letters left, and the plane
sound
echoed in his head at night. As if to register common nouns might
form a shape of empty time, freshening the scene, before becoming
instantly old again. Then lakes, masses, grains, delays, salvage
yards,
and rotaries appeared in the forms of words. With realization,
all things

are one family; with realization, all things are disconnected. The
separateness
of the fingers supports connectivity solutions, interoperability,
and a host
of client servers, all technical in their important, temporal
appurtenances
but of little impact compared to a single wave. From the selling
price you must
subtract the cost of goods sold to derive the gross margin. From the
gross margin

you must subtract occupancy cost; sales, general, and administrative
costs;
and any other costs of doing business to derive net profit. We live on
the margin. The gross domestic product is poetry. Otherwise, it's
fucking.
Looking out the window is incremental business. Reading from
books and games
on the floor represent growth, and at length there is tenderness,
understanding.

I like that dancing in the kitchen. It's the joy of it coming off
the floor. Trading is heavy on a volume of one hundred million

shares, according to radio eastbound 580 at High, and I recognize
that most of it's wasted on me but I hope you agree there's pleasure
in the exchange, box-step for theory for light, shaken nightly into

the human yard. Ropes, days, hammers, spikes, troughs, wars,
and bulletin boards of scraps of paper stuck to concrete kiosks
in muddy markets mark the way, an array in aggregate, a popular
contrivance at last. And that's not the half of it. Between what
goes in—unutterable instants turning the neck to rubber—and
        what comes

out—endless lists, taxonomies fraught with hype, latex covers that
        bulge
and stretch to contain, speaking peoples alive in the hood—there is
        a margin
of error, a float, a delta or difference, exceeding all limits by the
        sound of it.
Separations in space, yeah, you got an alternator all right,
right here in your up-to-the-minute breath supply, oh host. We are guests

on this planet for such a short time it would seem, and yet one
contains multitudes, mirrored universes receding into the ten
        directions,
loss leaders sparking close-out sales amid frenetic retail traffic, west
counterpoised against night, day in and half out of place, all well
defined at a moment of simple composure, as you turn back to the
        well.

Ice Cubes II

open
window
put
air

conditioner
on
words
it

doesn't
really
matter
which

ones
hanging
by
them

on
the
lip
of

existence
let's
just
relax

and
finish
our
wine

□

being
with
fire
being

with
water
being
with

trees
standing
still
for

long
periods
of
time

□

a
neutrino

would
be

extremely
lucky
to
hit

anything
while
passing
through

an
atom
scientists
say

☐

We
at
First
National

have
you
by
the

balls
I

remember
Evan

saying
in
New
Haven

□

there
are
no
people

in
the
centers
of

the
cities
at
night

only
a
few
conventioneers

and
tourists

drinking
quietly

□

work
chop
fades
out

under
the
windward
sun

parallax
blade
needle
wave

who
owns
the
sky

god
who
owns
the

earth
the

king
who

owns
the
ocean
we

do
said
the
girl

☐

why
is
a
woodnymph

a
good
character
to

have
the
words
have

to
come

from
somewhere

□

it's
sometimes
worthwhile
to

have
one's
subjectivity
examined

□

you
don't
subscribe
to

the
dream
channel
but

you
get
it
anyway

☐

there
is
a
dead

space
in
time
that

is
known
as
waiting

but
is
unknown
as

intelligent
life
on
Mars

you
have
to
go

outside
your
mere
expectation

you
must
be
warrior

□

the
avant-garde
is
our

home
away
from
home

□

Thursday
or
Friday
noon

looks
good

for
hoops

let
me
know
if

you
can
make
it

☐

bone
supports
flesh
but

what
supports
bone
animation

conspiracy
de
la
soul

☐

a
grain
of
salt

is
what
we
take

all
research
findings
with

☐

glut
of
this
world

I
have
imposed
sanctions

by
having
my
cable

removed
for
the
duration

☐

single
tack
pointed
up

chunk
of
coral
weird

bent
stick
red
rock

Hotel
Sovetskaya
lobby
pass

annotated
topography
a
bottle

of
pills
I
don't

have
to
take
anymore

☐

all
mind
is
available

only
after
hours
in

light
of
the
sun

☐

we're
always

looking
for

it
but
this
is

it
it's
very
disappointing

☐

I'd
like
to
have

one
of
those
lung

clocks
to
measure
the

rhythm
of

life
against

what
do
you
say

nothing
hurts
to
say

☐

the
camera
changes
everything

that
passes
before
it

☐

lines
cascading
down
years

place
coffee
on
glass

mustache
feathers
stomach
muscles

wry
grin
in
passing

☐

having
too
much
and

too
little
to
do

with
anything
the
crackling

hysteria
of
the
moment

intervenes
on
our
behalf

☐

item
it
is
still

raining
outside
item
my

foot
is
not
sore

item
we
are
part

of
an
ongoing
concern

this
kind
of
thing

happens
all
the
time

☐

breath
goes
in
and

out
heart
pumps
blood

to
brain
life
spills

over
into
night
streets

☐

time
to
step
outside

the
normal
course
of

events
take
a
walk

around
the
block
the

block
is
huge
the

universe
must
be
expanding

□

we
are
no
longer

in
possession
of
the

Omaha
Steak
Flyer
a

lurid
four-color
depiction
of

various
cuts
of
meat

⬜

I
have
the
sense

that
history
is
chewing

us
up
and
swallowing

⬜

a
light
breeze
another

day
a
deep
breath

a
heart
beat
is

a
unit
of
measure

like
an
ice
cube

☐

the
current
year
will

bring
you
much
happiness

I
can
believe
it

☐

birds
above

transmission
shop

on
South
Van
Ness

☐

sleep
deprivation
creates
a

sense
of
being
visited

by
someone
or
something

but
not
being
home

☐

THOUGHT
contains
non-contiguous
blocks

☐

I
don't
know
what

weapon
it
is
that

once
outside
your
doors

will
help
my
girlfriend

give
her
best
performance

□

wind
knocks
paper
cup

off
edge
of
ledge

it
bounces
and
rolls

in
a
wide
arc

scudding
against
the
concrete

□

dreams
seduce

memories
snag

leaves
tremble
water
collects

in
beads
on
leaves

☐

I
find
my
words

have
outlived
their
own

meaning
which
is
vanity

but
do

walk
standing

out
against
summer
air

☐

love
oh
love
oh

careless
the
tea
kettle

played
a
minor
seventh

The Person

For Lyn Hejinian

Increasingly, then, the person becomes a way of doing something, never explicitly experienced as such, because it is the world that is felt, its mute pressure filling out the corners, as of a rhyme. The room gathers each sitter in. The light changes, imperceptibly, always. One, the inevitable protagonist of a paragraph built on second thought, would like nothing better than to sum up and in the application describe that process by which so much detail has been set aside, so as to be clear of it, to stand in the pale light unframed by the body of years spent in collation. The assembly of days, none identical to the last, has taken up much time. So many sources, however, have informed the final mix, that it bears an irreducible mark, one not possible to describe in so many words. The person looks around and sees the same things. It is necessary to change without touching them.

Here a street or a sky or a bridge become emblems in an elaborate game whose rules the person is only beginning to understand, although an avid player since early childhood. Perhaps it is the availability of such images that prevents one from recognizing their true meaning until much later, when one has withdrawn or been withdrawn from them, through an illness or brush with death, but one has not had time for such things, or been spared them by luck. Mostly it is the call of others that diverts the attention.

If a child or a woman or a man or an old man or a young woman or a person of questionable age approaches you, what do you think? Many wish to first get out of the way. Others jump at what may seem like the main chance. The one particular person I have come to consider has thought rather to be of assistance, to the extent possible, in relation to this, that and the other thing, however. In this way, this person has become an extraordinary resource for a good number of people. What remains to be seen is a person, walking over a bridge.

What is of more interest, however, from the point of view of a junkyard of mangled signs heaped up in silent protest against a century devoted to the material possession of form, is when a person eludes any simple formulation relative to that interest.

The person is, as cliche-ridden isomorph, a creature of habit. One has certain convictions, obsessions, eccentricities, stylistic features, indications that set one, by prescription, apart. All this is begging the question, a delay tactic, for what most impresses its mark on the spirit, an insistence lived, a laugh in the face of horror, marks its presence without recourse to definition. It is the world that is felt, but it is a made place, and within it they make it who alter its composition simply by living and doing as they will and can do.

Transmission

Under all the symbols—
going out to eat, letters,
punctuation, full-motion video
there is life—indescribable, not
to be denied. And under
life—nothing. The gaps
wake us. Our only response
is practice, placing one
provisional step in
front of the other. Other-
wise, there's weather. The
hints sound like popping
rain. But no formula conveys
it; only tone does, a way no
logic sounds right that
stiffens the back, a back-
ground noise determined at
some point deep in the
ground. I guess you could
say, "We're working on it."

Leveling

Into the been, the wire, fleeting, scant,
because just enough space has been brought
forth, on account, strange, unfastened, about
to tip over in the occult, remaindered gloom
apart from a fist and a lemon batched
in time, the wholesome moment slags
then ripens and bolts down two thirds
of the standard operation known as once,
once more rising to the varnished, complicit
occasion. That complicated a sentence could
only be produced in a matter of monuments
criss-crossed against a dime folio, more
forgotten than accidentally picked up. The
shining genius in an hour, all four legs of the
bed planted squarely on solid floor, hoists
the tattered pennant of doing okay. By the time
this gets divested the concommittent aspects
collide, and there are wonderful packages waiting
in gradually darkened claim rooms at foreign
stations, a form of transport closely aligned
and in alternating venues policed, diced, cleaned.

Equanimity

The alternating blind alleys of tooting your own horn
and lapsing into dark humors may be avoided by going
straight to the light available in an escalating syntax
pronounceable only through sound, that agency whose office
serves up periodic reminders in the form of events, sun
bearing weight on the leaves, breezes just barely touching
the backs of the shoulders and legs, sky penciled in
at the last moment. A kind of free-floating anxiety
settles on a cornstalk then disappears over the fence.
How like a cartoon are the Tom-and-Jerry features
of this Sunday heatwave and radio Dizzy Gillespie
or Tito Puente backhouse day! There is a shuttle service
twisting in and out of the weather, which is like a message
for us to slow down. Philip Larkin listed as his
hobby, resting. Various other signals cross media paths
and cancel in the dynamic, portable air. Later
a gorgeous screen will be erected, luminous
with scenes of travelers traversing bridges under mountain
landscapes inlaid in mother-of-pearl, to announce
the concealment of something germain yet lacking
the temerity to declare itself, as tumblers are filled
with water in advance of the main meal. That something
turns and kicks its space gently into general circulation.
Weight, as in the weight of these words, coalesces around a
manner of speaking, charged up, occasional, and like France,
twice its normal size. By the time you get to the end of it
you are reminded of the very beginning, when so many shapes
could be made out in what later turned out to be the world.

The Messianic Trees

Happily gobbled
exercise book
collude as giddy
performative spurs
the thought embodied
spanking new
a doubt or drain
Paleolithic

Over the years
agitation
two minutes to go
the loop, the catch
hum of heat
back to back
being closed in on
isolation

Book matter
live with them
specimen days
for excellence
home to Harlem
the melancholy comic
but passion
be the spine
standing on edge
in this rattletrap radiance

the white guff violins
sham halter
the messianic trees

Softening beams
wistful terrace
harbor select
indefatigable

Affairs in order
latent animalcule
abutting dissonance
the whole way
cough of altered imagery
patina
trading fours
on the off chance
practicality

Deciduous
scattered
occasional
luminary
quixotic
non-plussed
canny
beast

Stun gun
why
barometric
salute

the feeling
outside language
on the curb
on a dime

Don't stop
bus life
adjust chair
waiting there in the sky
these things aren't what
simple pattern
citizens pour out
onto the streets

A day makes
settlement
fashioning wings
pornograph
well you needn't
industrial park
layabed
anthracite
the standalone sentiment

Dully moving
against the sum
facade
ligature
cataleptic
stanchion
as much light
tamed

the inner place
thriving

Loaded pieces
object linking and embedding
Ur-palaver
building America
glamorous heroes are attractive

I have your man here
his colors fortify me
I refer to schedules
incandescent blitz
farming the corridor
a slip of a girl
range and domain
apart
the universe is deep
but we are extremely wide

Donnez-moi un peu d'espace
atomistic practice

Three skies
paradigmatic
visible support
since '91
the whole motor surround
as easy as
ordinary mind
you can't find
because you'd be going against it

Three kayaks
coming toward us
the sun on the water
a shimmer
nothing further
and this nothing
reintroduces the proposition
an arch across space
time conglomerate
packaged to slide into a rack
the industrial nations
inventing childhood
in the image of obsolete commerce

The abstract beauty of buildings
aging in sun
indicates an ache
in the personal transmission
between what is there
and who says it is there
in their underwear
tree sections
apartment
roof
when I get there
turned out to be from the 70s
you flash so fast
scattered
and arrived on the same day
a map
from the 18th century
the look of references
squeezing

Local hero
commingling granite
antipasto
a laugh in the face
star line
bituminous
incendiary
wing flame halter
bathing in the bash
for likes
and a suntan maybe later
all contours of expression
revolve two houses
down in a banging sound
these words as obdurate
as that world we enter
alter

Borrowed venue
parenthetical sweep
pounding the building
into the concrete
stand up and go away
the motor dimension
handleable

What later readings
come away with
is no business
of this
ant patrolling
edge of desktop

approaching notebook
now climbed inside

Roll with the outsiders
the land of hush
stains it with laughter
colloidal
ambergris
blue poles from all the way back
as if another person
then sees it
fading toward afternoon
a light glimpse in a busy station
life shot through with
five sounds
convergence replication stamina
a field for tacticians
unavoidable
point blank
then I'll see you tomorrow

We don't want no Fascist groove thing
paste interior monolog here
street soup
got used to the word: supper
planks left from before
ruins mirrored in construction
we citizens walk
shadows cast at a cigarette angle
art patrol
what threads of the past
desire pulled through

plaid jacket hung flat on a door
wind sprints

Funnel situation
down to this
Lew Welch at the sink
a wisp of smoke in the sun
music wheels the membership
drawn flat against the side of high noon
Bill Monroe
thought the words: blue moon
sense minus time equals space

The terrific realism of
still sticks in my head
it will take all day
reducing things to essentials
then stretching the real skin back over
cool as ice
the quiet dignity of a former time

A peculiar deference
Brazil billboard chunk scape
every day
hands that cross waves into
light mid-morning traffic
said more than could
grasses and flowers falling
in the brave new world of power and light
business as usual is history

Lane violation
spontaneous strain

combustible
authoring tools
limited warranty avenue of
night vision
poles through mid-day lots
once empty
energy
the claim that stays

I think these stones
then make up my bed
tossing narrative
into sheet music
until the sentence is almost done
waiting here
for the third person
a tune heard once

Factory character
Chinese weight
total attempt to change
wherewithal
straight size
lazy parenthetical

Available now for the first time
crashing cinders
in an about-face voice
rush to tabulate the summer precinct
a handsome skin-tone or shelf-life
discovered subjectivity
pronoun relative to said facade

turned up later in bed
re: smooth member or matter
a wait that slides
particle haven on the eyes
one time only

Massive amounts of unstructured data
steep slope
getting up in the morning
the recognition engine
the character expert
the symbolism of juggling
the search for killer trees
growing a culture may take
a few hours to a few weeks
an eternity on the dough lines

You have a flair for
crystal gazing
insufferable
three sheets to the wind
mid-Victorian taco junket
rank lyricism
weasel word at the ready
but I
six concrete footings
cedar plywood embrasure
$979
have a railroad to run
uncomplicated
personal literary injury
and have a quatrain to broach
short circuit

I look at things a little different
along the z axis
sound action
followed by endless elaboration
the quiet in light of glint
the after speak
an open and shut case
you have to start somewhere
leaves move
two yards off
in sun
window displays
general parametric silence
in play

Pillow block
a journal and its bearings
a dense clump of grass
buoyancy espousal
my brain is by way of being mush
stymied
the unbearable penis of boring
face time
pillars of salt in reverse
the surrealist moment
in exchange for a lovely evening
lying prone
inside the mechanism

Polytheism
doesn't strike me as too much to ask
turquoise grabbers

elm

quay

tain

to write is to crawl through a narrow passage

to read to survey the wreckage

maximizing profit yields

at every feasible juncture

the voice of reason

Flexible digits

physical reality is jammed

between Plato's Forms & your & my perceptions

according to the New York Times

can't recall how short "short term" was

no recollection of how long "long term" was

crowd edging forward intermittently

pushes space pockets backward

my theory is

crisis pushes the pragmatist

in the direction of the visionary

my experience is

bus proceeds haltingly

through Friday night drizzle and exhaust

In the winter

we know which side our butts are vetted on

apple back into an eye

DNA is the computer

past tense

ambulatory

consignment

Triangular colors
way of life on hold
similar parameter
strange bright large and various darkened things
sound people
take flight
square it with the boss
half a mind flashes past
disrobe connected hammering
magic fashioning
harmony in the blood
she walks across the yard
anything is possible

Wonder what'll happen
spontaneous rubble housing lots
inside history outside time
percentages
cross-sectional sofa
a mere idea rubbed blank
against the curb of day
what powers have auspice to break the mold
once thought put in place
now bested by act
collision chain
aviary
consumption

As to what is
beautiful
contemporary
fleece

amber-colored
we are past it now
overlooking the little gold corner
it's hard to say
feelings coming through the wireless
patched over with sandy moss
a kept lantern
Boston stadium dragoons
not at all what I expected
rosary
recursive grammar
parallelism to burn
and place before you
before you get home
to surprise you
without knowing what to wear

Without the wear and tear
we'd be younger than that
to which we bear witness
but that
by which we are smitten
are the new buds
bursting onto the scene
as always
this script repeats itself
in one hundred thousand signatures
toppling totals
every instant

Train window instant youth serum
up and down the line

adrenal
Mayday
Pentax
softening against the hinge of earth
left to cool on the sill
my country
awake
in another county
narrowly missed by now

Bouncing back from
when you least expect it
harmony
closed off on one side
that's the limit
a stimulant
white glare off the floor
speculation
systematic blast furnace of an afternoon
temporizing

Old nickel
hardware coupon
dynasty mesh salute
moving per capita
cautionary
big-time
handsome and extremely shy
in a time zone
reportedly
with one hand tied behind
rent-free

time of day
lit magic

Disaffected
intransigent
banish
happenstance
solely
argumentative
watershed
heat
you have two moments
to make your case
birth
death
and a window of opportunity
open on
fields rushing by
woo woo

Ghost traps
caravan
in descent
topiary
extraction
yarrow yellow
way station
crippling blast of
sentimentality
harbinger
roll bar
camouflage

high in the stirrups
I mean you could go there
see for yourself

Role play
unintimidated
bad air
barriers to entry
the same result
spatula
betting man
without warning
the fix is in
nailed to a shrine incineration
unquote
I tell you
my pivot foot did not move

The whole story
gobbled up
in short takes
that faze
trailing sparks
that land
every so often
on the plot line
seen upside down
as stars
waiting to be born

Not knowing
not explaining

not repeating
just sitting
waiting
for the garbage trucks of morning
thus the twentieth century caves
in around the edges
in anticipation of night
the long seminar

The formulaic
leaning into the future
empathy
glancing off flower beds in light
purple cattails thriving
urge
contained in light

A single iron rail
ten thousand miles long
fall to the ground
get up from the sky

The Wall

The wall comes up
and you hit it
fall to the ground

Get up from the ground
head into the wind
here comes the next wall

You hit it
and so on
dust yourself off

Disentangle from the flickering light
register events
going off at a record pace

Next wall
you pass through it
recording charges for in-process research

And development
every day there are issues
exactly

You feel as though
the world were by way of being
about substitution

Charged up
buried
scattered with the wind

Standing amid the ruins
of a collapsed wall
standing and eating

Sleeping and making love
thinking it over
in the shadow of a wall

Moving like a fullback
into the line
making contact with it

Cloud Water

It's a human universe & we
pay lip service to the stars
typos in the genetic code

Inevitable
it's a big pool
language doesn't live here any more

Don't stick to any particular style
Listen to the other side of the words
Dragons and elephants, give me your questions!

The Sieve

Communicating vessels
let the outside in one ear
and out the other

In reference to history
the curb bangs against the wheel
the treaty has been replaced by the deal

Mixed metaphors
arrive after hours
folk music is deeply curled

A memory like a sieve
can be used to rinse vegetables
in the future

The Break

Timing is everything
you make your own luck
or so they say

Being in the right place
at the right time
by moving around enough it may be perfect

An opening in the clouds
weather is just there
what have you

what have you not
the tide floats all boats
joined at the hip to chance

Lolligagging in the brain stem
the homunculi
maybe hatched a scheme

Star schema language
enables machine-readable nights
weighing the pros and cons

The outlet pass
the assist
the easy score

Those nights in the 80s
of practice
at St. Elizabeth's High School gym

The X rays were negative
the colored balls scatter
across the green table top

Bright exemplars
of the laws of physics
skilled practitioners

Stroking them into submission
in Detroit
light winds

Messing up the surface
an opening in the forest
symbolic logic

Raw unfiltered honey
the sun is a moving target
an image enters the gate

Film is the truth
24 times per second
think fast

As they used to say
on that job repairing sprocket holes
for the maker of "Don't Look Back"

Or that completely different time
in the swing room
or smoking outside in the lot

Is that a fact?
yes it is
oh, so that's what a fact is!

Spinning on the pavement
like a human top
taking it from the top

There's a break in the action
consciousness
wants to stay awake

I'm indestructible
said my uncle
then we watched "Robocop"

Writing by flashlight
because the power went out

The Crave

An imaginary tune
breaks rocks
on the sound of time

Progressing syntactically
across 88 keys
it's not what I see

It's what I don't see
I don't see an end
I can't play in a world of infinite keys

The semblance of a mode
notwithstanding
the cloud is approaching the shack

They dropped bombs on the giant eyeballs
the line drops
like two movies spliced together

In a room
motor sounds image the thought
way out west

In time for a word
touching the body with light
one key at a time

A lick
a promenade
arrival

In time
all knees and elbows
the deck tips

On a sea of change
a sea of absolute sameness
with the alacrity of an accountant

Happy to be of service
aboard this stately world
of no nationality

Correctamundo

I'd like to write
a little bit
about the time

I switched to lit
my verse has an open architecture
many meanings can plug into it

Like business services
such as payment, tax, logistics
advertising, planning

And collaboration
but I'd like to say a few words
a television is the sun

My papers are all in order
pages turning
like the hands of a clock

Before all being
means publicly
in front of the whole universe

That's a H-O-R-S-E shot right there
it must have been the adrenalin
from behind the backboard

Get it first
but first get it right
in the same way it was

Like "April in Paris"
by Alex Chilton
with its triple ending

charging through the font
charging through the font
of repeatability

The 4th of July

A seven-minute poem
is written in the time
it takes to cook two hamburgers

On the grill
you get up and check your drink
make sure the hamburgers are not sticking

And check your watch
the hamburgers have been cooking
for about three minutes

Light is coming from the sky
flip the burgers
spill book odd pieces of paper

The sun is setting
behind the fog
check drink

Not bad
slim chance of any given event
all held together

Like a rose
about to burst
onto the scene

30 seconds over Tokyo

Line 56

Hey, poetry lovers!
it's good to see you
here on the page

The white spaces
are looking good
today, huh?

Hey, I gotta admit
I'm not too clear on
what all the different

Things are that I'm actually
doing with you guys
I think maybe we have Bill

S. speaking at your
show in England or
something like that

Even though
we never met
we can still get along great

We just take life
one line at a time
with a nod to the past

And an eye to the future
from the exact point
where they meet

This mobile integer
that flickers between zero
and one

The Gap

Penumbra halter top commissary
simply the greatest
numerous pictures explain

The rhyme in the prison hatch
staring out of bounds
to a tune flow symbolism

All my connected joineries
Sing this song
Battle haven newco phenomenology

Sports injury interoperability
claiming long distance
in halves of laundry light

Car box television
in leavings off
in swing

That I had to tell you
when you were not here
this is my song

With music in the backfield
short tight patterns
on the air

Separations in space
that blow your mind
are waiting to be organized

In abandoned railway stations
Crazy Kat and Ignatz
hitting him with a brick

While Offica Pup naps
under a cactus moon
two frames left of the gutter

Pre-TV heebie geebies
rattle my skull
but it's all right

My machine sings
because it is plugged in
interwoven memories are placed into circulation

Unconscious bugs
flat in time
paranormal nebula pajamas

Slanted over their backs
Phoenicians on ships
shepherds awake in the mountains

Three sixty video chill
bridging the gap

The Outcome

When I was a musician's musician
I used to be a poet's poet
then a black box

Turned off the alarm system
according to the script
at this time the outcome

Is unknown
and I
am a professor of indeterminacy

In collaboration
with my trusted business partners
the birds

Who inhabit this hillside platform
enduring the confused status
of a forklift upgrade

They sing and I
merely stare at apples
and occasional other fruit

Citrus combine of this belated orchard
in Little Romania
next to where water

Cascades down steps that lead
to something not immediately
identifiable as such

A febrile dog
ripping the hell out of
an inflatable wading pool

Such are the pleasures
of Little Romania
the sky

An unvariegated deadpan blue
the mild undertone of desolation
dusted with erotic chimes

It would be foolish to think
and I have no intention
in keeping with this interoperable crepuscule

We are open
the advent of standards is a boon
hail to the salt in our wounds

We hold these truths
faster than speed
it never entered my mind

Here in midsummer
the day is long
the train sound recoils in the hills

Every bit of mental ice
is used up
in the emotional juice we drink

And words mean nothing
and the movies suck
less than our heart's desire

More than you ever know

Le Meridien

French swells
with their razor-thin toupees
have adorned these chambers

With their French-poodle cartoon attitudes
reverse engineered
to produce ephemeral critical effects

Relatively distinct
from the rather unprepossessing corporate offices
of outlying suburban hamlets

In order to form a more ruthless taxonomy
on the order of fat onion soup
and its impression on the taste buds

Even in absentia
whereas glistening streams
repeat an audio circuit

Lost above Tetonic wilds
I have lost my place
in this parthenogenetic afternoon

Of long words, fluorescent light
hitting the baseline of a scratch
claw hammer deliberations

Over popular cosmetic long odds
I guess you could say
fabulous you could say

Shoulder tops square with the horizon
purposefully fogged and slagged
in the manner of Doc Holliday

In his late period
tipped measurably sideways
into an erstwhile nobility

While counting the cards
of an un-intermittent if
hardly conscious desire

Wax riffs smooth the imaginary legs of time
pealing off singles into memorabilia
dear old stucco

Where did you go
old semaphore
fading into integral absolutes

Down the line?
or only into academic ethnicity
freaking the bejesus out of Beverly Hills

And yes I have been true as
well as inestimably false
anything pure is weak

The days have their own way of being
to which we contribute
next to nothing

In the big picture of things
that hangs in the projection room
during a film by René Clair

In which three top hats
land sequentially on a lawn
of an afternoon

Far from Salinas
and the yellow metal sombreros
of Claes Oldenburg

The Didn't

The sky is bright
is a matter of opinion
resting beside a day

Location penumbras
click against
what's already bought in

I get a kind of
sideswiped diligence
from years of yard work

When I look at you
it's not that there aren't already
many key signatures to hang out in

But the chords that last
century left us
ought to have their notes tightened

The bay is flat
is a custom condition
sandbagged toward sunset

Totality balloons
pop every
second thought

The terrible silences
of the World Bank
chip at the noisy rainforest

We turn to the Biblical splendor
of colorful images
when we watch the Olympics on TV

These data were collected
by the only means available
random interception

Braced with momentum
charged with history
in a moment of absolutely not

The sun is invisible
at this hour
and in this poem

Because the book is closed
pages are flush
and the night is quick

As hand and eye
tumble into preconception

Walnuts

In poetry
you are given all the letters
and have to arrange them yourself

On a wall
in the next episode
you are a married couple with kids

Going between three houses
to pick up stuff
along a narrow stair

You are glad to be out of there
invigorated, unencumbered, hopeful
passing by the window of another

Man who knows you
roughhousing with a massive, naked bald woman
her husband comes in and says, "Walnuts!"

The sea is the color
of poetry
as defined in a guide

To leading questions
left out to dry
in the sun

The fish live under
the sign of the pelican
in a sea of answers

Not written in any book
the kids went back up to the house
you taste rock

And the salt stings your eyes
20 Spanish mackerel
in point of fact

Your pen is leaking water
like newly real details
of the world at large

The Music Lover

He has fallen asleep and is sleeping
earlier I thought I
heard him saying something

But this was not the case
he had fallen asleep
and was sleeping

Later I could have sworn
I saw him
moving surely across a room

Perhaps I was mistaken
since he was already asleep
and had been sleeping

For some time
his presence continued to make
itself known to me

Even though he was asleep
and sleeping peacefully
on another level

It got to where
I could ask him questions
about his perspective on life

And he would seem to answer me
despite the fact
of his having fallen

Asleep, of his
continuous and effortless sleeping

9:45

3:15

The immediate impulse
claimed
in a light fog

East Bay
of night
I alter nothing

Save the sound
of walking later
through these leaves

29

You labor around
the corner with various
ideas of what

You get confused
between work
and family dynamic

It's all too much
as are you
as dear as you are

Imitating a whirlwind

$1250

Whether you gave her
first and last
and a deposit

Or whether the last
was the deposit
that is the question

3VBH351

We are rapidly and successfully
ramping up
on several continents

He has a long road
ahead of him
with a lot of curves

It is very, very beautiful
I'm glad I lived
long enough to see it

30

You have 30 new messages
7 are urgent
I've heard it said

30 points
and 10 rebounds
was my career high

At the bottom of the copy
to indicate the end
—30—

7′ 10″ x 10′ 10″

Not $2700
she paid $2400 *each*
argument over a $60 lamp

Hand mower
sense of scale
Pannonica

Noon
hour of the smallest shadow
pandemonium of all free spirits

528-5030

Veined conferencing
in the speeded up architecture
of behavior

Urban sprawl
when on the weekend an instance
flees the scene

Concision accelerated
through the inflection point
meaning flipflops

150,000 Sq. Ft.

We have people stacked
on top of each other
the new place

Will give us plenty of elbow room
I don't want to be a bottleneck
I'm going to lie down

On sofa number two
leave the lights on all night
scare the raccoon

I

Call the station agent for a message the
elevator project
track I

Sound of cars whizzing past
approaching train thunk
bike gloves black mesh

Lines are interstitial
under ground
on arrival

The basis of the week
excite at home

2

I played two
lost two
and scored two

And that's counting by twos
the speed of light
and the span of life

The water-spike mountain
in between
is being leveled off

88.5

Mind forms
chug across
the ocean of sensibility

Increasing production
50%
by next year

760

Used up time
doing what?
open your eyes

Open your eyes
oh, my!
the road bends

Oh, my!
the road bends
doing what?

Absolutely
time to go
a user's manual

50

Things are getting serious
kum-bai-yah
it's time to settle the score

Don't get mad
get even
Lee Van Cleef

I've never had so much fun in my life

200

JFK's back hurt
I'm moving
retroactively

Jesse Jackson opening a FedEx
out front
the Shangri-La

Just a few minutes ago
I'm feeling
as they say

Almost human
it's a nice day for it

27

The heart itself
contains genetic instructions
to like certain things

Pros like Jay don't need tips
you don't refuse to breathe, do you?
I leaned against the door and breathed

A word of it
and waited for my heart
which was now full of new information

212

You were right
I was wrong
go back upstairs

And get back to work
he isn't ready yet

10/30/99

Late heat in fall
music of sky bug release
dream come

Sun dust
banging the air
up against the drugs

Screech of Saturday light
impressionable

8

The mind loses track
somewhere after 6
although the count continues

In the background
what is the background?
it looks like infinity

As in Vince Edwards
sitting zazen

1.5

Take a risk
with one and a half sticks

MM

Millennial hoohaw
a nit
in geological time

Now you see it
now you download it
ulp!

Anything, anytime, anywhere
out of this world
at the speed of light

5:32

In between time
is the right time
to be

With the one you love
who do you love?
train sound

Loudspeaker echo effect
it's been a long time
it won't be long now

R566JPH

The eternal return of the slightly different
oh yeah
put it right over there

You're going to burn
a nice little hole
in your Baudelaire, my dear

White man speak with numb tongue

5:08

Whether you're a hero
or hanging on by
your fingernails

Awake when not
degree of difficulty
opportunity to fail

To sleep
perchance to creep
good luck finding your hotel self

Keeping several balls
in the air

7:52

Camden light
cranks of the shaft
glass of water

Sum twist
skis of the last
supernumerary

Convincing you of
the rhythm of surf
allover cicada tubular

49

American movie classics
the channel I was born on
year of Parker, Pollack & Jack

Not Pop Warner Brothers
but studious
in the long shadow

Of WWII
hands in pockets
heads down

Whistling on the way to work

28-023

The ice flows
break up
until all hours

Simply by being
the compression
of incremental change

Scratching the surface
hatching a scheme
batch processing

The holy names
out of the living daylights

24

It's been 24 days
since the surgery
24 x 7

Was how I worked before
it's the 23rd of November

Thanksgiving Day

Storied fate
daily mind
wooly bully

2001

Negative vision
computer subplot
psychedelic pap

Breathing in space

99911

54-40
101
18

With a bullet
six o'clock
straight up & down

Cash money
because because because
Fashion Island

Pack my snoot
I'll be up
in a half second

14696

Bill Evans
"My Foolish Heart"
like an afterthought

In space
the Bay is a fact
To remember

Plug in all the lamps
and rejoice in light
of everything going on

All the time
tonight we live
on Darius Way

52

Double happiness
means happy right now
and happy in general

Stanzas for an evening out
past the spike
and the precipitous after-drop

We will either be irrelevant
or heroes, one